I0624100

Before the West

The First Light on Unknown Lands

Hamid Ran

Edited By
Roop Wazir

Copy right

To the Quiet Angels of My World

There are countless people who have touched my life, lifted me through the hardest moments, and walked beside me during every step of my journey. So many souls have helped me, supported me, and changed me in ways I could never fully express. If I were to name each one of them, it would fill tens of pages. One day, I hope I can write their stories too, how they shaped my heart and my path.

But for this first book, I want to dedicate it to the roots of my life.

To the souls of my father and my brother.

To the most patient and kind person I know, my beautiful mom.

To my brothers-in-law, my nephews, and nieces: Abbas, Majid, Kasra, Saeed, Mehdi, Shabnam, and Maryam.

And above all, this book is dedicated to the angels of my life, Azam and Zhaleh, my sisters, who are everything to me.

For ten years, you have cared for our mother with endless patience, compassion, and love. You gave up your own time, comfort, dreams, and rest to be by her side every second of her difficult days. Even when her dementia has brought confusion, anger, or pain, you have stayed gentle. You have stayed kind. You have stayed devoted.

None of this would be possible without your husbands, your children, and everyone who stood with you in this journey of love.

Azam and Zhaleh, my dear sisters, this book is dedicated to you.

My heart, my gratitude, and this book, everything I am, belong to you.

And my heartfelt thanks to Roop Wazir, whose care and editing helped bring these pages to life.

When the Train Pulled My Heart Away

I was scared. I was nervous. I hated unknowns, yet now I was walking straight into the heart of many of them. I was about to see my closest friends without knowing what to say. I hated goodbyes. I wandered the streets, looking at shops, houses, and salesmen pushing their handcarts full of cooked broad beans. My eyes were wide open as I tried to memorize every single inch of those streets. My head was spinning and spinning, though no one could see it. Even in the crowds of people, I couldn't hear anything. I never knew I could feel so deaf, though, of course, I wasn't.

"Hey, Mr. Reza!"

My friend shouted it so loudly that it snapped me back into reality. It was getting dark, and I had only a few hours left before falling into all the unknowns ahead. I hurried to buy the last item on my list: two boxes of cigarettes. I had been told cigarettes were expensive on the other side of the world. I stuffed them into a black plastic bag and carried them carefully to my room so I could hide them in my luggage. I never smoked them in front of my family.

I packed my entire life into one red suitcase and one black backpack, the same backpack that had been with me through every uphill and downhill, every mountain and forest. Just looking at it triggered so many memories; my mind drifted back to all the places it had traveled with me and every single friend that joined me on those trips. I couldn't stop thinking about them. I stared at my suitcase and my backpack, as my eyes grew wetter and wetter.

"No, no, no. You can't cry," I kept telling myself.

I was in my tiny 130-square-foot room in the basement of my parents' house, sitting on my single bed with a blue metal frame that had been with me since middle school. A small carpet lay on the floor. The only carpet I have ever truly loved. The walls were covered with pictures of nature, photos of my parents, and portraits of poets I admired. A small desk and a bookshelf filled the rest of the space. Being in that room made memories flood into me, like days and nights spent with my friends in that little room, away from my parents' eyes, drinking and laughing.

Was I going to miss all of this?

Or was I actually relieved, happy even, to burn every bridge behind me and step into a new life?

It was going to be a long night. I pulled myself together and went upstairs to sit with my family. I needed to say my last words to them before leaving.

There were two rooms upstairs, both considered living rooms. The smaller one had the TV, and my parents slept there. Whenever my sisters, my brother, and I were all together, we always gathered in that smaller room.

No one knew what was about to happen, no one except me. My family had no idea that this might be the last time I ever sat with them in that room. They thought I was simply going to Turkey to attend university and continue my education. But deep inside, I knew the truth, and keeping it to myself had felt unbearable.

There was no future for me in Iran anymore. The Iranian government had become more and more suspicious about me, keeping me under their watch. I knew I couldn't stay.

So I was leaving. Forever.

It was almost impossible to tell them. I loved my family to death, every single one of them, and saying goodbye felt like ripping my own heart out. I hated goodbyes. This was the first goodbye in my life where I had absolutely no idea what waited for me on the other side of it. It was hard. It was so hard.

And yet, something in the air felt different that night, as if everyone somehow sensed what was coming. The whole house felt heavy. We were all unusually quiet, not like other days when we laughed, played games, and talked for hours. That night, no one was speaking. We just sat there, watching TV, but not really watching it.

Time felt strange. I don't know if I was rushing or if I wanted the night to last forever. I couldn't tell if time was flying or crawling. I kept glancing at the clock on the wall, then looking down at the carpet, then back at the clock again. I was confused, nervous, and overwhelmed. Everything was unknown, and this was the first time in my life that I was leaving my country with no plan to ever return.

We were all gathered in the room: my parents, my two sisters, my brother, my two brothers-in-law, my three nephews, and my two nieces. My nieces were still little and wouldn't understand anything, but I already knew how much I would miss them. All of them. But especially my nieces. No one said anything. There was nothing left to say.

My instinct kept telling me that my brother was the saddest one in the room. I didn't know why. I never asked him, and I still don't know whether what I felt was true.

Time kept passing, and every minute brought me closer and closer to the moment I would have to leave. With each second, I felt more anxious and more scared.

My cousin, his wife, and their son came to say goodbye. They didn't know anything either. We were so close that I called all my cousins my brothers and sisters. We grew up in the same house when I was a child, and they were already grown. They said their goodbyes and left, and suddenly, reality hit me: I was truly about to leave my home, with thirty-one years of roots and the city where I was born and raised. And the house that I would forever call home.

My friends came to pick me up to drive me to the train station, where I would leave Iran for Turkey.

Before departing, we hugged, and we kissed each other, my whole family. On the way, I sat in the back of the car, quietly crying. Normally, it would only take about five minutes to get from my home to the train station, but I asked my friend, who was driving, to take me through the middle of the city, through downtown. I wanted to see downtown one more time, one last time.

As soon as we arrived at the train station, I saw my brother waiting for us. And not just him, my other friends were there too. I then spotted something else: a few Iranian secret police agents standing around the station, watching us.

At that time, the Iranian government had this attitude that if someone they considered a threat decided to leave the country, they would be happy to see them go, and they wouldn't interfere. But I didn't know if these agents were there because they were pleased I was leaving… or because they were frustrated they never managed to arrest me, imprison me, or do whatever else they had planned. Either way, their presence tightened something inside my chest. My anxiety doubled. My nerves burned.

I said goodbye to my brother and my friends. My friends knew I was leaving forever, and that made everything even harder. But the time had come. The train was waiting. I had to board and begin my journey.

One thing I knew for sure: it was going to be a long journey, full of unknowns, full of waiting, full of new experiences I couldn't even imagine yet.

I said my final goodbyes, stepped onto the train, found my seat, and cried softly.

A Storm of Questions

It was almost midnight when I boarded the train. The carriage had beds, so I opened mine and laid down, but I couldn't sleep. I tried so hard, but my mind immediately drifted into a storm of thoughts with a million questions spinning through my head.

I kept going back and forth with myself:

Did I do the right thing?

Should I continue on this journey?

Should I go back?

Then another voice inside me whispered:

No... the future is bright. Something new is waiting for you. Keep going.

And again, right after that, my doubt returned:

But what about my parents? What about my sisters, my nephews, my nieces, and my only brother? What about them? What about my brothers-in-law? My cousins? My friends? All the people I love to death? Will I ever see them again?

My mind wouldn't stop.

I still have time. I can still return. I don't have to leave. What can the Iranian regime do to me? Will they put me in prison because I wrote articles they didn't like? That's fine. I'll be in prison for a few years. I'll survive.

But then another voice shouted inside me:

Are you crazy? Look at how many young people have lost their whole lives in prison. And how many were tortured, how many came out with mental and physical scars that will never heal from. You're lucky you didn't go through that. Don't go back. Don't ruin your life.

I was so confused.

But no... I can't go. My roots are here. Thirty-one years of my life are here. My thoughts wandered back to everything I was leaving behind, and fear held on to me tightly.

Where am I even going? Do I know what I'm doing? Even if I leave Turkey, even if the United Nations accepts my case and I go to another country, how will I learn a new language? I'm thirty-one. How will I find a job? What will I do? I always wanted to be a writer, or a teacher, or a journalist. But it will take me years to learn a language well enough to write again, or to do anything that I love. Maybe it's better to go back.

The whole train ride, memories and worries tangled together. I kept thinking about every possibility, my past life, my current situation, my future.

And on top of all of that, I wasn't in a good financial situation. My friend Majid helped me to get a loan.

My original plan was to use the loan to buy a car and work as a cab driver, because the regime had told all Iranian newspapers and news agencies that they were not allowed to hire me. I couldn't be a journalist anymore. And I didn't want to go back to welding. So, I thought, okay, I'll be a taxi driver.

Then I remembered: I couldn't even do that. At that time in Iran, one of the requirements to be a taxi driver was to be married or engaged. I was neither.

Therefore, I used the loan to skip Iran. I left a small portion of the loan money with my parents so they could pay it off until I got somewhere and could send money back to them. To this day, they have never allowed me to pay them back.

With all of that running through my head, I stared out the window of the train, thinking about my life and all the uncertainties ahead, wondering where I would live and whether I would ever see beauty like the mountains of Iran again.

I didn't sleep.

By around 6 a.m., we reached the border. The officers collected everyone's passports. They gathered us all into a hall and started calling names to return the passports with the exit stamps. I felt my anxiety rise again. I still didn't know if I was making the right decision or not.

They called everyone. Finally, the only other person in the room received their passport. Five minutes passed, five very long minutes, and still no one called me. My heart was pounding. I was sure they had kept my passport and were planning to arrest me.

When I finally stepped forward to grab my passport, the border officer suddenly appeared in front of me and, to my shock, spat at my feet. At that moment, I knew I had made the right decision. I was certain my journey had to continue.

I was going to miss Zanjan, the city where I was born and grew up. Thinking of my city brought a soft sadness to my heart. Of course, I was going to miss Iran, the places I had been, the mountains, and the New Year trips with my friends. I would miss them deeply.

When I was a young man, I was a mountain climber and part of a group that founded a mountain climbing club called Everest. Starting that club was one of the most memorable things in my life. Now, thirty-one years of memories were carried in my heart and my mind, and the distance felt even heavier.

We used to say that Zanjan had nothing to do and nothing exciting. But now, as I traveled farther from the city, I realized I was going to miss every part of it, like the historic places like Sultaniyeh and Rakhtshooykhaneh. I was going to miss the street between Chaharrah and Saadi Vasat, where we used to walk up and down all day, or at least two or three times a week.

I was going to miss my family and my friends. I was going to miss the newsletter we started. I was going to miss my editors and my colleagues who worked for that little publication. I was going to miss some of my coworkers from Iran Transfo, where I worked as a welder. And I was going to miss my mountain climber friends dearly; we were so close. So many mountains together, including Damavand, the highest mountain in Iran, at about 5,800 meters, and Sabalan at 4,800 meters. We climbed Alamkouh at around 4,850 meters, the same mountain my uncle died trying to ascend. It's one of the hardest mountains to climb in Iran. I climbed them all with my friends, and every one of them holds memories I'll never forget.

There's a saying among Zanjanians: "We don't know what Zanjan has, but whoever lives there finds it hard to leave." And I felt that. I knew I was going to miss the city.

It was a mix of feelings, a constant duality of emotions. On one hand, after everything that happened to me, when they handed me my passport and spat in front of me, I was relieved that I had chosen the path to leave. On the other hand, I knew I was leaving behind things I loved. And as these thoughts returned to me again and again, I kept asking myself the same question: If I go to Turkey, and then to my final destination, will they ever accept me as a citizen? Or will I always be considered a stranger, a guest?

A New Land, A Borrowed Sky

The train journey continued until we reached a city in Turkey called Van. The train couldn't go any further. From here, I would have to take a ship to reach another city and from there continue my journey by train to Ankara, where my friend Davut was waiting to host me, and help me begin my process to apply for refugee status with the United Nations.

The ship was not a cruise people took for vacations, and honestly, it didn't even feel like a real ship. It was small, dirty, and crowded. Inside, there was a kind of saloon, almost like an amphitheater, where they had set up plain plastic chairs, which were not comfortable at all. In front of the chairs, there was a low stage where a DJ was playing music. People were drinking alcohol freely.

Coming from Iran, where drinking or selling alcohol is strictly forbidden, it felt surreal. It was chaotic, loud, strange, and somehow, it was also my first real taste of social freedom. I didn't know whether to feel happy, sad, shocked, or surprised. It was as if two worlds were colliding inside me: the world I had just left and the one I was entering. The idea that I could simply walk up, pay money, and legally buy a drink was not possible back home.

I wanted to get a drink and go sit on the ship's patio, to watch the open sea and the stars. It was nighttime, and the idea of quietly holding a drink while looking at the sky felt poetic to me. But I didn't let myself do it. I told myself that from now on, I had to be careful. I was on my own. Every penny mattered. I couldn't take risks, not even small ones.

So, I didn't get a drink. I just sat there listening to the DJ, trying to take everything in. And again, I don't know what happened to me, so I started crying. When the emotions became too much, I walked out to the patio so no one would see. I sat alone, watching the stars, feeling the cold air on my face. But still, my mind wouldn't rest.

Thought after thought after thought.

Did I choose the right path?

Will everything be okay?

Am I going to regret this?

Will I miss my family? My friends? My home? Even the food?

What will become of me? Where will I end up? What will my life look like?

I have always hated the unknown. I still do. The unknown makes me anxious, nervous to the point where I feel it physically. And this journey was nothing but unknowns.

It was my second night without sleep. I was still sitting on the patio, staring at the dark water, when suddenly the sun started rising from the very edge of the sea. It felt like the world was slowly turning on a light just for me. I pulled out my camera immediately and captured the moment. The sunrise felt like a blessing, like a message that maybe, just maybe, good things were coming my way. That kind of beauty gave me hope.

No Longer Home, Not yet Safe

An hour or two later, we disembarked, boarded another train, and continued toward Ankara. When I arrived at the Ankara station, I called my friend Davut. He told me to take a taxi and to hand the phone to the driver so he could give him the address. When I arrived at Davut's apartment, he was already waiting for me outside.

Inside, the home was full of people. They were cooking Abgusht, a traditional Iranian dish made with chickpeas, tomatoes, potatoes, meat, and onions, with a few variations depending on who makes it. You drink the broth separately, then mash everything else together and eat it as another dish. The smell of it filled the whole apartment.

Seeing all the people in Davut's home made me feel less alone. It reminded me of home, of gatherings, of the comfort of being around other Iranians. For a moment, it almost felt like I hadn't left at all. It gave me a small sense of hope that maybe this journey wouldn't be as lonely as I feared.

The next day, Davut took me to the United Nations office by bus. When we arrived. We saw there was a long line outside. Most of those waiting appeared to be Iranians, particularly Bahais, who are persecuted by the regime and face countless restrictions in Iran, from being barred from university to being excluded from government work. Like me, they had chosen the refugee route.

As we waited in line, a small detail caught me off guard. Birds roamed freely among the people, pecking at food on the ground as if they weren't afraid. You don't see that in Iran, where people usually chase animals away. But here, the birds looked relaxed. That tiny detail stuck with me, as if even the birds sensed they were freer here.

Eventually, the doors opened, and we walked in. I wouldn't call the United Nations staff rude, but they weren't friendly either.

Their tone was loud, rushed, almost like shouting instructions in all directions. They handed out forms, we filled them out, and they told us to wait until they called our names.

When my turn came, the interview was very short, just basic demographic questions and the reason I wanted to file for refugee status. Based on that, they decided where in Turkey I would be required to live. They told me I would need to go to Niğde, a small town, and introduce myself to the police department there. They also gave me my official interview date with the UN, almost a year and a half away.

I left the UN office and now had to take the bus back to Davut's home. My mother tongue is Azeri, half of Iran speaks Azeri, and because Azeri is similar to Turkish, Turkish is supposed to be easy for us to learn. But I didn't know a single word. It was only my second day in Turkey. And whenever I don't know a language, I become shy, nervous, and scared to even ask a question. I was terrified that I might take the wrong bus. Thankfully, I didn't. Davut had explained the route very clearly, and I managed to get on the right one.

On the bus, my mind started racing again. The future stretched in front of me like a long, dark road. I kept thinking about the long journey ahead of me. First, I would have to wait over one whole year for the UN interview. Then, after the interview, there were more months of waiting to hear whether my case would be approved or not. Then, another interview to assign my final country of destination. After that, more interviews with the embassy of that country. It felt endless.

How would I survive until then? I didn't have enough money. I had no support. I would have to find a job, find a home, make a life, all in a place where I didn't speak the language. The thoughts kept circling: Will I survive? Will I have food, shelter, and clothing? What is going to happen to me?

By the time I reached Davut's home, my nerves were exhausted. Davut helped me get a bus ticket for the next day to go to Niğde, a 4-5 hour ride from Ankara. I stayed one more night at his home and left the next morning.

Taking buses in Turkey turned out to be much easier than I expected. They had small shuttle minibuses that picked you up from near your home and took you straight to the main station. The bus station was clean, organized, and very modern.

And the bus itself, unlike the filthy ship, was extremely clean and comfortable. The seats were soft and spacious, and they offered snacks and drinks several times during the trip. I still couldn't sleep. I can never sleep on a moving vehicle, bus, plane, train, or anything. So, I stayed awake, watching the scenery.

Turkey is beautiful. Green hills, wide fields, mountains, it felt peaceful, almost healing. Yet behind that peace, my mind whispered, reminding me of everything I still had to face: a new city, a new life, starting from zero. Immigration is like being born again, except your "experience" is the only thing you bring with you. I was 31, but I felt like a newborn.

Life on Hold

I arrived in Niğde, checked into a small motel, and spent the night. The next morning, I went to the police station and introduced myself. They wrote my name down in a notebook. I had to go there twice a week to sign and confirm that I was still in the city.

I started looking for a place to rent. In Turkey, real estate shops are small storefronts, and I visited many of them. The language barrier made everything difficult; I barely understood them, though they seemed to understand me better. But everywhere I went, I heard the same thing:

"You're Iranian and single? We can't rent you a place."

I didn't know the reason. I didn't even know the language well enough to ask. Every day I went from shop to shop, and every evening I returned to the motel disappointed and hopeless. Each night, I lay down on the motel bed, wondering if I had come all this way just to get stuck in limbo.

I called Davut again and told him everything. He contacted one of his friends, who had connections in Niğde through two university professors. They also tried but heard the same thing. We finally learned the reason:

Many Iranians in Turkey stayed up very late, held loud parties, and disturbed their neighbors. So, landlords were afraid to rent to single Iranian men, assuming they would cause trouble.

I felt crushed. Again, the same thoughts came back: Did I make the right decision? What will happen to me? Am I going to survive?

Then I remembered a friend from my hometown, Zanjan, who lived in Kayseri, a nearby city. I thought maybe he had connections.[1]

I called him, told him everything, and he said he knew someone in Niğde who might help. A few minutes later, that person arrived at my motel.[2]

When I met him, I felt a positive vibe. Without saying much, he grabbed my luggage and said, "Let's go."

"Where?" I asked.

"You're coming to my home. I live with my son. You'll stay with us until you find a place, or forever if you want."

I told him I had already paid for the motel that night and wanted to be independent, and I needed my own place. He refused. He insisted that finding a place wasn't easy, and I couldn't stay in a motel forever.

So, I checked out and followed him to his home. I met his son and the cat they had rescued from the street. Seeing how they cared for the injured cat told me everything about who they were: kind people.

That night, after dinner, he said there was a coffee shop where many Iranians gathered every night. They played live music, served tea and coffee. He suggested we go and maybe ask around for housing.

I didn't love the idea. I didn't want to stay in an Iranian circle because I wanted to learn Turkish, and community comfort slows language learning. But I had no choice, I needed a home.

---

[1] The reason I don't name him in this book is because I have no connection with him anymore and cannot get his permission to include his name.

[2] Again, I won't name him because I cannot get permission.

We went. We drank tea, listened to music, and slowly, I realized I was falling in love with Turkish music. I had never liked it before, but now it felt warm, emotional, and familiar. In that small coffee shop, surrounded by strangers, I felt a strange mix of homesickness and belonging.

While we were sitting there, a young man approached, greeted my friend, and sat with us. His name was Aydin. When he began speaking Farsi to me, I was shocked; his Farsi was perfect. I later learned he was Turkish but spoke several languages fluently, including Farsi.

When he heard I had been a journalist, he asked if I could help him understand some poems by Hafez. I told him Hafez is difficult even for us, but I would try, and maybe he could help me learn Turkish in return.

I told Aydin about my situation, and he said one of the real estate shop owners knew him well; maybe going with him would help.

The next day, we went to the same shop that had already rejected me. But with Aydin beside me, everything changed. They said they actually had an apartment available, and I could move in anytime.

I was so relieved, finally, a place of my own.

Aydin took me to second-hand shops to buy furniture, dishes, and basics. He also sold me some of his own items, like a bed. Slowly, I built a home.

Once I moved in, Aydin helped me set up utilities, internet, and everything else.

Now, a new chapter of my life had truly begun. For the first time since leaving Iran, I wasn't just passing through; I had an address.

The next urgent step was finding a job.

The apartment I rented was far larger than I needed, but it was the only option available, so I took it. It was a three-bedroom apartment with one full bathroom and one small restroom. The heating system was unusual for me: I could either buy an electric heater or use charcoal. The place had a big hall, a large living room, a huge kitchen, and an enormous balcony. It was on the fifth, and top, floor, with no elevator, tucked right behind the police station.

The rent was 250 Turkish lira, which at that time was about $208. It was expensive for me, but again, it was my only option. I thought about getting a roommate, but at the same time, I felt that having a roommate, especially another Iranian with the shared culture, might somehow take away my independence. I furnished the apartment as simply as I could: a couch, two armchairs that were yellow and black (I really loved them, they were beautiful and comfortable, and Turkish furniture in general is well-designed), a dining table with four chairs, and the bed I bought earlier from Aydin. I furnished only the living room and one of the bedrooms.

The water heater also ran on charcoal, unless I bought an electric one, which I couldn't afford. It took me a while to learn how everything worked. Getting on the internet took some time, too. I didn't even have a smartphone, just a Nokia flip phone. To have internet at home, I needed a landline, and that was also the only way I could talk to my family. In 2008, there weren't many apps for video calling, or maybe they existed, and I didn't know about them. I would always talk to my family once a week by phone.

Slowly but surely, I began getting used to my new place and to Turkey itself. The culture was close to ours, and my neighbors were amazing. There was another Iranian family in the building, but we only had passing interactions, saying hello, small chats, nothing more familiar. My neighbor across the hall, however, was incredibly kind. When they realized I lived alone, and since I was always quiet and careful not to disturb anyone, they would sometimes bring me lunch or dinner. They were such a nice, generous family. Their kindness softened my loneliness a little.

Days passed while I waited for my interview with the UN. I had already contacted Reporters Without Borders and received a response quickly. They told me they knew me, had read my articles, and could confirm that my life had been in danger in Iran. They contacted the UN directly to support my case. Two days after their email, I received a call from the UN informing me that my interview date had been changed, from one year away to just a month and a half. I was over the moon. After weeks of stress, anxiety, and overthinking, it felt like finally, something good was happening. I knew there would still be long waiting periods ahead, so I continued looking for a job.

Around that time, I met three Iranian men who were roommates. One of them didn't even have his own room; he was sleeping on a couch in their apartment. He asked if he could be my roommate, and I said yes. He moved in and took one of the bedrooms. Not long after, we both found a job in a factory that did many different things, basically handyman work. With my welding experience and his general skills, they hired us. We agreed on a wage of 20 lira per day, about 10-12 hours of work. It was an under-the-table agreement because we didn't have legal permission to work in Turkey. Turkish workers were getting paid 50-70 lira a day, but we didn't have a choice but to take the lower wage that was offered.

We started working, but in time, our employer began refusing to pay us on time. He would pay us for one day, then skip paying us for five days. Then he would pay us for one more day and skip another six. It was humiliating and stressful. I finally reached a point where I had to stand up for myself. I threatened him, saying that if he didn't pay me, I would report him to the authorities. He didn't take me seriously at first and told me to do whatever I wanted. I had noticed they were stealing electricity, so I decided I could use that against them.

I quit and told them they had until the next day to pay me the 300 lira they owed, or I would report them to the electric company. The next day, the owner's son brought me only 150 lira. I refused and demanded the full amount. They promised to send the rest with my roommate that evening. My roommate was still working there, and they were supposedly paying him. That evening, he brought me another 50 lira. I never received the last 100 lira I was owed.

I was constantly worried about how I was going to pay the rent, cover my bills, and afford groceries and daily expenses. At that point, I knew I needed to look for another job.

I received a call from a nonprofit organization called ASAM, the Association for Solidarity with Asylum Seekers and Migrants. Their agent in Niğde called me, introduced himself, and told me he was also a journalist. Because of that connection, he asked me for a favor. He said an Iranian minor had just arrived in Niğde and needed a safe place to stay for a few days until a permanent arrangement could be made, and asked if I would host him.

I agreed. I told him the boy could stay with my roommate and me for a short time, but when my family came to visit, I wouldn't have room for him. He understood. A few days later, the minor arrived. His name was Majid, and he had a lot of connections with other Iranians. Because of that, he quickly found a job for himself and for me.

We started working as welders in a village outside of Niğde. Every morning, we had to take a minibus, about a 30-45 minutes ride, arriving around 7 a.m. We worked until about 7 p.m. Even though the pay was still only 20 Turkish lira a day, the employer was an incredibly kind man. He always paid us at the end of each day, and he provided breakfast and lunch.

And the breakfast, Turkish breakfast, is honestly one of the best in the world. Dozens of dishes: fresh bread, olives, eggs, potatoes, cheese, butter, jams, different omelets... so many delicious things that you could sit and eat forever. We would work for about an hour, then go to his house (the workshop was attached to his home) and have breakfast with him and his family. He made doors, windows, roofing frames, and all kinds of welding jobs. The work was hard and tiring, but we enjoyed it because he genuinely took care of us, and his family was just as kind.

In the evenings, we would come home, shower, and sometimes go out with friends, to a coffee shop or just walking around. Even in small cities, the nightlife in Turkey is lively and full of energy. Life was slowly moving forward. I wasn't stressed about money anymore since I was working regularly. I was waiting for my UN interview, and also waiting for my family to come visit. They still didn't know the truth about my situation. They thought I was in Turkey to continue my education at a university. I wasn't brave enough yet to tell them that I had left Iran for good, that I was seeking asylum, and that my life had changed forever. I kept everything to myself.

Eventually, the time for my interview came. I bought my bus ticket and went to Ankara. I stayed the night at Davut's home, and the next morning, I went to the UN interview. It was extremely difficult, four hours long, with a break in the middle. The UN officers (they called them "lawyers") were incredibly knowledgeable about Iran: the political situation, religious minorities, LGBTQ issues, journalists, everything. They asked very detailed questions, and I could tell they were trying to find any inconsistency, anything that didn't match their knowledge, so they could deny the case. It was intense.

Before the interview, Davut's friend Nader, an amazing person, truly one of the kindest people I met, helped me organize all my documents. I had brought all my published articles and materials from Iran, but I had hidden them carefully. I had put them in the back panel of my backpack, covered them with fabric, and asked a shop to sew it shut, just in case Iranian authorities searched my bag during my travel. No one would have been able to find them.

Nader helped me sort everything, translate the article titles into English, and prepare a clean file to give to the UN officer. That organization helped me a lot during the interview.

After the interview, they told me they would contact me by phone, or I could check the status of my case online on a website they gave me.

That interview was not the end of anything. It was only one gate I had passed through. One mistake, one inconsistency, one sentence that didn't match what they already knew, and the entire case could collapse. If they denied my case, it wasn't just a "no." It meant going back to waiting, waiting without a country, without protection, without knowing if I would ever have a normal life again. People think refugee status is something you simply "get" if your story is true. But the truth is not enough. You have to prove it again and again, in rooms where every detail is tested, and you have to relive the worst parts of your life as if you are on trial endlessly.

What makes it even more difficult is that this interview, a few hours long, can change your entire life, either in a good way or in the worst way. You walk into that room already exhausted. Your anxiety is already skyrocketing. Imagine a job interview, then multiply that stress by a hundred. In a job interview, if you fail, you lose one opportunity, but other doors remain open. You apply again. You move on. In this situation, there are no other doors. This is not even the finish line; it is only the beginning, but it is a beginning that carries enormous weight. And while your body and mind are overwhelmed with fear, you still have to be fully present, fully focused, careful with every word, making sure you don't make a single mistake.

They say that if your story is true, you won't make mistakes. But it is not that simple. It is not only about you. One sentence, one word, one misunderstood detail can lead to misinterpretation and change everything. Years of waiting can be thrown away in a moment. I was lucky, because of the support of Journalists Without Borders, I waited only a few months for my interview. Many others are not that fortunate. Without support, people wait for years and years, suspended in uncertainty, with their lives on hold.

I returned to Niğde and continued my normal routine, working every day, going home, and checking the website every single night. Nothing changed. The same unchanged status every day. I couldn't do anything except wait.

About six months later, I was at work cutting iron with an electric angle grinder. My phone rang. I recognized the number immediately; it was a UN number. I was terrified to answer. What if they didn't approve my case? What would I do? Appeal? That could take years. My hands were shaking, and I just let the phone ring. Majid insisted I answer it. He pushed me to face whatever the result was.

I finally picked up.

It was good news.

They had approved my case!

I was so shocked and happy that I accidentally cut my finger with the angle grinder. The blade was extremely hot, so the cut didn't bleed; it burned. It was deep, but I didn't care. I was so happy to feel anything. When we got home that evening, we went to our usual coffee shop where many Iranians gathered. One of them was an Iranian nurse. I showed her my finger, and she said it was fine, no stitches needed. "You're young, it will heal," she said. She was right. It healed perfectly.

That night was one of the best nights of my life. For the first time, I knew I would have a final destination. A country would accept me. I could start my life again.

While I was waiting for the next step in my refugee journey, I was enjoying my life in Turkey. I had a job that allowed me to pay my bills and cover all my expenses. I was independent, and the culture felt close to mine, the social freedoms, the warmth of the people, the kindness, the friendships I made, and even a girlfriend whom I still love to this day, even though we could never be together.

Days and nights passed, and I kept waiting to hear back from the UN, wondering what my next step would be.

During this time, my sister called me and said, "Tell me the truth. You didn't go to continue your education. You left Iran forever, didn't you?"

I asked her how she knew, and she said one of our neighbors' daughters had told them.

I said, "Yes. I left forever. But I can't tell our parents. Please tell them for me."

She said, "Don't worry. I'll talk to them. Everything will be okay. We just want the best for you."

I didn't know if I was sad or relieved. For the first time, the heavy responsibility on my shoulders felt lighter. My sister's voice comforted me, but I was also terrified of my parents' reaction. We are very close as a family. As the youngest, I knew it would be hard for them.

But I had no other choice. I told my sister to tell them everything, that if I went back, I had no idea what the future would look like for me. I didn't know if I would be free to be with them or in prison because of my writing. She promised she would talk to them, and she did.

Soon after, they decided to come visit me. I was over the moon. I was going to see my family after months. It was one of the best pieces of news I received during my time in Turkey.

Their Visit, My Breath

They came by train, my parents, my sisters, one of my brothers-in-law, one of my nephews and his wife, and my two little nieces, who were very young and unbelievably cute at the time. (They still are cute to me. I still see them as babies.) The train didn't go all the way to Niğde, it stopped in Kayseri, so I hired a minibus and went to Kayseri, picked them up, and brought them to my apartment in Niğde.

The two-hour drive in a minibus from Kayseri to Niğde felt as though it passed in a second. I couldn't stop talking. I kept asking about everyone, how they were doing, and what was happening back home. I was already missing my brother, my other brother-in-law, my nephews, and my entire extended family. My cousins, my aunts, and my uncles. I loved them so much. I hoped that one day we could all gather together again, just one more time, and have fun like before.

I kept asking about everyone, even the neighbors. We laughed; we talked. They brought so many Iranian snacks that they knew I loved. They started opening the bags right there in the minibus, feeding me like a baby, as if I had been away for years, even though it had only been a few months. That is what happens when you belong so deeply to your family. They become your belonging, and you become theirs. And that time, those moments together, became one of the most valuable times of my life.

As soon as my parents stepped inside my home, they took a deep breath. They realized I was okay. They had imagined I was suffering, homeless, or living in terrible conditions. I'm not saying life as a refugee in a host country is easy, it absolutely isn't, but I was able to manage it. And honestly, I loved Turkey. Everything about it.

I learned the language very quickly. One thing that helped was reading children's books in Turkish and translating them into

Farsi. I translated nine books for my nieces and sent them notebooks. They loved them.

As soon as they arrived at the apartment, they started unpacking. They had brought so much food to cook, rice, ingredients, Iranian tea, everything they planned to prepare during the days they would stay in Turkey. At that time, the culture had not become westernized yet. These days, it feels much closer to Western culture, but back then, if you were an Iranian single man and your mother and sisters walked into your home, you had only one role: to sit back and let them do whatever they wanted.

They rearranged my kitchen, changed everything, and started cleaning, deep cleaning. They fed me like a baby, no matter how old I was. And I wasn't allowed to help. Cooking? Not at all. Washing dishes? Rarely. I had to beg them just to let me do something, but my sisters wouldn't allow it. At that time, my mom was still healthy and not sick at all, and that made me so happy. I knew I was about to eat real homemade food, my mother's food. Even though I had left Iran only a few months earlier, I already missed it deeply. I was excited. I wanted to relax, enjoy the moment, maybe help a little, but no matter what I said, I had to stay quiet and let them take over.

My roommate was happy too. He joined us and enjoyed the Iranian food, so he was more than satisfied.

That very first night, as soon as they walked into my apartment, they started making tea and preparing dinner. It was a great night. Two of my nephews didn't come with them. They stayed back home to keep their shop open and running. They ran a small grocery store, not like grocery stores here, just a very small version of one. So, they stayed behind. My sister was constantly worried about them. Did they eat? Did they have breakfast? Lunch? What did they eat for dinner? Every time we talked to them, she questioned them about food, food, and more food. Did you eat? Do you have food?

I'm sure she had cooked a lot before leaving and filled the refrigerator so that they wouldn't be without food while she was away. That's how it is in traditional families like mine. Maybe it has changed now. I don't know. I haven't been home for almost eighteen years. But at that time, that's how it was. Mothers were always worried about whether their children had eaten, even when those children were no longer children at all, but adults who could take care of themselves.

My brother and my other brother-in-law didn't come. My brother-in-law couldn't take thirty days off from work, and my brother simply never left Zanjan unless there was an emergency. The only time I remember him traveling was one trip we made with my cousin and his family to the north of Iran, and even that felt like a miracle. I still don't know how he agreed to come.

The other times he left Zanjan were only for serious reasons, like when my father was hospitalized in Tehran. Otherwise, he never liked to travel. He preferred to stay home. Honestly, I was angry. I wanted to see him. I missed him so much. Sometimes I felt it was selfish of him not to come and visit me. But at the same time, another question kept coming back to me: how was it not selfish of me that I was the one who left all of them behind?

While my family was in Niğde, we spent beautiful days together, walking, shopping (my sisters loved shopping), laughing, and eating delicious food my mother and sister cooked. My father had an incredible sense of humor, and every night we laughed so much. Even my roommate enjoyed their company. Those days felt like a small island of peace in the middle of my very uncertain life.

My mom is the quiet one. She is the most patient person I have ever seen in my life, and she is well known for her patience throughout our entire family. Everyone says, "We've never seen anyone who can be patient at this level." She had a tough life, especially when my brother was in the military during the Iran–Iraq war. For several months, we had no news from him, nothing at all.

One day, one of my brother's friends came to our home. He knocked on the door, and when my mom opened it, he told her he had seen, with his own eyes, that Iraqis had arrested my brother and cut off his head with a knife. Right after hearing that, my mom had a stroke. Thank God the news wasn't true. My brother was alive, he hadn't been arrested, and eventually we found him. One of my cousins, who was also doing his mandatory military service and worked in a sort of call center for the army, was finally able to locate him after months. My mom finally talked to him on the phone at last.

Her time in Turkey, there were two things she wanted: to hug me, and to say all the comforting things mothers say to their children, treating me like her baby, even though I was thirty-one years old. And of course, she wanted to cook my favorite foods. They brought tons of items from Iran just so she could prepare my favorite dishes. Another thing she absolutely loved in Turkey was the farmers' market. The only thing she wanted to buy was those traditional vests that Turkish aunties usually wear. She fell in love with them and bought a whole bunch. She never complained about anything, she was quiet and calm the entire time, but I still don't know if she felt the same way inside.

My sisters have very different personalities. My older sister is like my mom, patient, quiet, never complaining, keeping everything inside until it becomes too stressful. She is kind, sweet, and wonderful. She has three sons. The oldest one and I are only five years apart, so it doesn't even feel like an uncle-nephew relationship, although he still calls me uncle. She is a housewife who loves to cook, clean, work nonstop, and take care of everyone, including me, treating me like a baby no matter how old I am. She also has a daughter-in-law now, since her oldest son got married, and both of them were with us on this trip.

My younger sister, who is older than me, but she's the "younger" sister because I'm the baby, is different. She has my father's personality. She is direct and straightforward. She takes everything easy, she's calm, she's kind, sweet, and she loves helping others. But just like my older sister, she still treats me like her baby brother. She has two daughters, my nieces, who mean the world to me. It's not that I don't love the others, but in Iranian culture, daughters are often a little more spoiled and protected, and we adore them. They were both with us on this trip, and they were just the cutest, most adorable girls. Likewise, my other sister is a housewife, but she likes to go out with her friends, have fun, and support her daughters.

My brothers-in-law are calm, respectful men who mind their own business and are always kind. One of them is self-employed and owns a grocery store; the other worked in the treasury department in Iran before retiring. They have similarities and differences, but one thing I appreciate is that they don't treat me like a baby. I have a great relationship with both of them. But on this trip, only my older sister's husband came; my younger sister's husband wasn't with us.

My father was the funniest one. Every night, he made us laugh so hard. He had this cute, innocent sense of humor. One of my nephews, the middle one, is tall and big, so my sister always bought large clothes for him. And my dad was short with a little belly, and he never wore jeans; he was always a suit person. But every night, when my sisters laid out everything they had bought during the day (an Iranian tradition I'm not sure exists in other cultures), my dad would try on the oversized jeans, coats, and shirts meant for my nephew. He would put them on, stand there in the biggest clothes you could imagine on his tiny body, and start dancing. We laughed so much during those nights. Those silly dances are some of the memories I hold closest to my heart.

My oldest nephew, the one who came with us, has his own strong personality. He tends to complain about everything, but honestly, sometimes his complaints make sense. I don't blame him. He is still a good kid, and his wife is incredibly sweet, a perfect fit for our family. She is kind, polite, and warm-hearted.

And my nieces, I can't say enough about them. They were everything to me on this trip. Whenever we went out, I held their hands, and we explored everything together. My little niece was very young at the time, always jumping around, excited about every little thing. She was just adorable. My older niece was in elementary school then, calmer and more thoughtful. She had a mixture of her father's and mother's personalities. Both of them are extremely close to me. The little one was very attached to her mom, so at that time, the older one was closer to me. These days, both are equally close to me; we talk regularly, and our bond is still strong.

Some of my friends invited my family for dinner and lunch, and my parents truly saw how kind the people around me were. It meant a lot to me that they could see with their own eyes that I wasn't completely alone.

One day, one of my friends invited my entire family, along with two other families, for dinner. He had prepared a huge, fancy meal for all of us, and he really went above and beyond. After dinner, in Iranian culture, whenever there is a gathering of more than a certain number of people, maybe fifteen or so, it almost always turns into a little party. We don't just sit and talk the entire time. We usually play music and dance, and it's one of the most enjoyable parts of our culture.

So, after dinner, they played music, and oh my God... my dad danced nonstop with everyone, kids, adults, women, men. He was unstoppable. He loved dancing, and he danced with every single person who pulled him onto the floor. We were all joking with my mom, teasing her, saying things like, "Look at him! He's dancing with all the young women!" And my mom just laughed and said, "Let it go. He's fine. He doesn't mean anything." She was sweet and calm, as always.

On another day, one of my other friends invited my entire family again, along with the same families, for an Iranian kebab picnic in nature. He prepared everything for us. It was beautiful. We spent the day outdoors, grilling kebab, eating together, playing music, and dancing again. I remember taking so many pictures that day. We laughed, we relaxed, and we had so much fun; both days were unforgettable. Likewise, this friend of mine went above and beyond to make this happen.

Every single moment with my family felt precious. And the whole time, deep inside, I knew I was going to miss these moments terribly. As I watched them laugh and dance, a part of me was already grieving the goodbye I knew was coming. I kept wishing that one day the Iranian regime would change so I could go back home freely and have these kinds of memories again with my family and friends in my own country. To this day, that wish still hasn't come true.

After a few days, we decided to travel to Istanbul so they could catch the train from there back to Iran. We flew from

Kayseri to Istanbul, and we spent several days exploring one of the most beautiful and incredible cities in the world. My family loved it.

My little niece, who was too young to understand things, kept saying, "Here is not abroad. Niğde is abroad. Let's go back to Niğde!"

She had no idea how funny she was.

I needed police approval to travel because I had to sign the notebook twice a week, but the officers approved it immediately since my family was visiting. The police in Niğde were very friendly, polite, and professional. Some even became good friends of mine.

And then... the moment I never wanted to come: the goodbye.

We hired a van to take us to the train station, but my family insisted that I say goodbye at the hotel instead of going with them. So, I did.

My father hugged me so tightly and cried so hard, harder than I had ever seen him cry in my life. It broke me. When they left, I went back to my hotel room, fell face-down on the bed, and cried loudly. I cried so loudly that someone knocked on the door to make sure I was okay.

At the time, I didn't understand why my father cried like that. But later, after he passed away, I realized he knew. He knew that was the last time we would ever see each other.

Before Everything Else

My family's visit pushed me back into my life back to where everything first began. Now, all of my childhood played out in front of my eyes. Even though I don't remember much of it, I still remember some things. I remember snowy, cold days in my hometown, Zanjan. I remember my plastic boots with the very warm socks my aunt knitted by hand, the ones that kept our feet warm through the freezing Zanjan winters. I remember my fights with my sister. I remember playing with my friends outside. I remember my sister's friends gathering in the alley, playing some kind of drums, and we would all dance. I remember all of those days, even though they are blurry and the details are gone.

But I remember one day that probably changed my life forever.

Traditionally, in my family, education was a strange word. My parents were 100% illiterate. My younger sister was the only one in my family who got her high school diploma. So, I was the next hope. But on the day that changed my life, I was in the second grade of elementary school, and I had to have surgery to remove my tonsils.

Usually, in Iranian culture, at least in my family and among our neighbors, people would bring you a small gift after a surgery. But the gifts were usually fruit, ice cream, or simple treats, not even toys, just small things.

We had a neighbor right across from our home, a very educated family. Some of their relatives were even political activists, I believe, at least at that time, but I'm not 100% sure. What I do know is that they were highly educated.

When they came to visit me after I was discharged from the hospital, they brought me two books. I remember one of them for sure, it was The Ugly Duckling. The other one, I don't remember the name. But I was so happy. I don't even know why. I can't explain exactly what made me so happy to receive those gifts, but I know one thing for sure: it was the very first time in my life that I received a book that was not a schoolbook. It felt unique. It felt special.

I immediately started reading it, and I had my sister read those books over and over for me. It was such a crazy, beautiful moment for me. I was over the moon. Finally, it wasn't fruit or ice cream or pastries. It was something different. It was a book. And it was the first time I understood what a book truly meant, a book that wasn't for school, a book that didn't come with homework…it was a book that was simply… mine.

Finding My Voice

After I received those books from my neighbor, my habits changed. I used to get pocket money from my dad every day, and we were supposed to use it to buy something to eat at school, because at that time, schools didn't provide snacks or lunch.

My dad would give me pocket money so that during breaks I could buy something to eat. And part of that money, I had to save to buy clothes. It wasn't like the Western world, where you can go and buy clothes anytime you want. For us, it was only once or twice a year, right before the Iranian New Year.

I started exploring bookstores during school breaks. There was a tiny bookstore close to my elementary school inside the Zanjan bazaar. It was a very small shop, probably two meters by three meters. I would go there just to look at the books. Instead of buying food during break time or saving for clothes, I went to the bookstore and bought books. This made my dad upset. He never punished me or anything like that, but he didn't understand the value of books at that time. He didn't know how important they were. Later in his life, he understood. For him, the priority was to feed ourselves and save money for clothes.

But there was my brother, kind, generous, and remarkable. Even though his own education ended by elementary school, he understood the value of books. He understood learning. He supported me fully and always encouraged me to study. In Iranian culture, we believe that education is the path to reaching something higher in life, and he held onto that belief deeply. He always told me to spend the money Dad gave me however I wanted, never questioning it, never holding me back.

He would take me to his friend's shop, who owned a sports clothing store, so I could get shoes. And he would take me to another friend's shop in the other bazaar in Zanjan to get clothes.

There are two bazaars in Zanjan, both old and historic: the Upper Bazaar and the Lower Bazaar.

I preferred wearing clean, repaired clothes rather than torn ones, but I still saved money to buy books. Buying books had become my new habit, and I was happy with it.

As I grew up, I fell even more in love with books. Even though I didn't do well in school, I read many more books than I ever read from my school textbooks. Some of my school grades suffered from this habit, since all I cared about was reading and enjoying my books.

When I was in the fifth and last grade year of elementary school, we had a teacher who was addicted to hard drugs. He wasn't a friend of my father, but he knew him. I think they had grown up in the same neighborhood or something like that. So, my father, with a kind heart and not knowing any better, thought that if he helped the teacher with some money, the teacher would teach me better. But my poor father had no idea that his money was being wasted. The teacher wasn't teaching me anything. Instead, he was just giving me high grades that I didn't deserve.

There was one thing I didn't know back then: in Iranian schools at that time, we had three rounds of exams, and the third exam was the most important one. You couldn't get extra credit or makeup grades for it. It was the same in the last year of middle school and in the last year of high school. The third exam wasn't prepared by the school or the teachers. The questions came directly from the Ministry of Education.

Because I didn't know that, and because I thought my teacher would "fix my grades" again, I didn't study for any of the exams. And of course, I failed, I think in four or five subjects. I had to retake all of them during the summer in order to go to middle school.

That was when I found out the truth: my teacher had never taught me anything, and my father finally realized that he had just been giving me fake grades. My father was so mad and upset. So, I studied hard that summer and passed all those subjects to go to middle school.

Middle school became a new beginning in my journey with books.

Middle school was completely different because now, on my way, right in the middle of town, there was a bookstore called Chamran. It doesn't exist anymore, but back then it was a special place. Many people would stop by to see the new arrivals, talk with the owners, or just chat with each other. The owners were political activists, so the bookstore naturally became a gathering place for open-minded people.

For me, it was a whole new world.

Even though I was still young, in middle school, I fell in love with psychology. I started reading every psychology book I could find. The owner of the bookstore was shocked and always asked me, "These books are for adults. Do you understand them?" And I always said, "Yes, I love them." Every time I went there, he would show me the new books they had brought in, and I would explore all of them. I always read the first few pages, and if I liked the book, I bought it.

It wasn't just a new chapter in my reading life; it was a new chapter in my life itself. Through that bookstore, I met people from different backgrounds: writers, journalists, political thinkers, and young people like me who were curious about the world. I felt something new, a different kind of comfort, a new level of joy. I spent some of the best moments of my early life in that bookstore. I would stop by every single day, even if only for 15 or 30 minutes, before I had to run to my dad's shop to work after school.

Around the same time, something else happened. I was a huge fan of a soccer team, and because of that, I bought sports magazines that came out weekly. I believe they were published every Saturday, which, in Iran, is the beginning of the workweek since Friday is our weekend. The funny thing was, if you weren't at the magazine stands early in the mornings, you wouldn't get a copy. So, I used to give a little extra money to one of the shopkeepers to hold a copy for me until noon. I never missed an issue. I bought every single one and read everything about soccer. I wasn't very interested in other sports, only soccer. And slowly, through those magazines, I became familiar with journalism. It all started there, with sports magazines.

At the same time, my older brother-in-law was reading lots of newspapers. Every day, he bought two or three newspapers. He also read many books, though I don't remember which subjects he preferred. This, too, was another reason I became more and more involved with books, magazines, and newspapers.

During this time in my young adulthood, when I was reading books and falling in love with them, a family member gave me a gift, a Russian film camera. At that time, there were no digital cameras. The brand of camera I received was Zenit, a very famous camera in Iran during those years.

I started taking pictures. Of course, they were very simple and not professional at all, but I loved them, and I found myself falling in love with photography as well. I even remember that I photographed my sister's wedding and some other family members' weddings and birthdays, not for money or anything like that, but simply because it was a hobby I enjoyed.

I was always so excited to take the film to the photo shops to get the pictures developed. Back then, we didn't know how the pictures would come out because there was no way to see them ahead of time. And sometimes, if you made even a small mistake, like loading the film the wrong way, all the pictures would get ruined, and nothing would come out from the entire roll.

Those films usually came in 12-, 24-, or 36-exposure formats, and you would buy whichever you needed. In the middle of the city, there was a photography shop that printed pictures. I still remember its name to this day, Jamili. It was the most famous shop back then. We would take our films there, and they would develop and print them. I don't know if that shop still exists or not, but I know that back home in Zanjan, there are many modern photography shops now.

Photography quickly became another hobby of mine. I was so proud of my camera, because not many people had cameras in those days. I loved showing it off and taking it everywhere I went. Sometimes we went on school picnics with classmates and teachers, in middle school or even high school, and I would always bring my camera. Everyone would beg me to take their picture. It became another chapter of my life, and I didn't realize at the time how important it would become later. It was just something placed in my path, and I started shooting pictures without knowing what it would mean for my future.

Later, I bought a smaller camera, a Japanese brand called Yashica. My brother gave me the funds for all of it. I was lucky to have an older brother who supported me in these things.

On a warm summer day. I was working in my dad's shop, and my dad had gone to the capital, Tehran, to buy items for the store. I was alone. Whenever I didn't have customers, I would continue reading my books. My book was on the metal desk my dad used, which had two drawers. One of them we used as a cash register. It wasn't anything like what you see today. There were no bank cards or anything like that. Everything people bought was paid for in cash. The other drawer was larger, and my father used it to keep snacks, small inventory items, and things like that. My father was very smart, but he had never gone to school, so he didn't know how to read. I would write the inventory lists for him. Sometimes he would recognize items just by looking at the shapes of the words, and he would update the inventory himself, and most of the time, he was right.

On that day, I was sitting in the shop, reading, when a customer came in. Usually, we had regular customers, people who owned mechanic shops, tire shops, or handyman stores. We didn't get many strangers.

I put my book upside down, cover facing up, pages down on the desk, so I could go back to the exact spot where they left. Everyone who came in usually spoke Azeri.

This person spoke Farsi. That was unusual. Almost no one came into our shop speaking Farsi. He bought something, and then he looked at the book on the desk and asked me, "Who is reading this book?"

I said, "I am."

He looked at me, in complete shock and surprise. "You?" he asked.

"Yes," I said. "I'm reading this book."

The book was called Father, Mother, It Is Our Fault, in Farsi, Pedar, Madar, Ma Mottahamim. It was written by Dr. Ali Shariati, who was a psychologist and a modern Muslim thinker specializing in the psychology of relationships. But at that time, when I was in middle school, his books were considered political. Some of them, maybe most or all of them, I don't remember, were forbidden. People bought them from under-the-table markets, and if the government caught them, they had to pay heavy fines.

The man asked me, "Why are you reading this book? You're so young. I don't think you understand it."

I said, "I do. I understand it. It's easy for me to read and understand."

He shook his head and said, "Everyone your age is reading books like Young's Why." That was one of the trashy books that middle school teenagers read at the time, books mostly about sex, with no meaning. I had never read them. Honestly, I had only heard about them. They were shallow books with no depth.

And here I was, a middle school boy, reading Shariati.

He left the store in awe.

But I was terrified. Scared to death.

As soon as he walked out, my mind went in many directions. What if he is from the government? What if he comes back with the police? What if they arrest me? What if they take the book? My mind was going in a thousand different directions. Should I hide the book? Should I burn the book? Should I leave it alone and keep reading?

I was a teenager. I was shaking. My face was red. And all of this was because of a book.

Then I started thinking, what if my father finds out? A million questions were running back and forth in my mind.

My dad came back in the evening when it was time to close the store. We closed the shop together and started walking home. It was only about three minutes, maybe even less, to get home. But those three minutes felt like three hundred hours for me. I kept thinking about everything that had happened that day. What if that man comes back tomorrow and tells my dad something? What if he comes tomorrow with the police? What if they arrest my dad?

I was so worried. I was nervous. My anxiety was through the roof. It was one of those crazy moments that I can never forget in my life.

When we got home, I couldn't even eat dinner. Everyone kept asking me why I wasn't eating, but I simply couldn't. I made an excuse and said, "Oh, in the evening, the neighbors and I bought fresh bread and cheese, so I'm not very hungry." But the truth was that I wasn't eating food; I was eating my anxiety. I was so nervous I could barely hide my shaking. I had no idea what tomorrow was going to bring. I went to bed that night with a heart full of fear.

The next morning, I went to school as usual, and at noon, I went back to the store. When I walked in, I saw another book sitting on my dad's desk, another book by Shariati, called Kavir (in English: Desert). I immediately asked my dad, "Dad, what is this book doing here? Whose is this?"

My dad said, "Oh, I'm glad you asked. A gentleman who speaks Farsi came to the store and said he is leaving Zanjan, but he wanted to make sure you had this book before he left."

Oh my God.

I was over the moon. I was so happy. Suddenly, it felt like a thousand pounds had been lifted off my shoulders. I finally understood that the man was not a threat. He was one of us. He was someone who cared about books, too. And he brought me one of the most difficult books Shariati ever wrote.

But I was excited, so excited to start reading it.

After finishing the other book, I began Kavir. I read the first page... and I couldn't understand anything. I was just a teenager. I read it again. Still nothing. I read it again and again. It was so heavy. I wasn't able to understand it at all. I got tired and frustrated, so I decided to pick another Shariati book to help me transition into this heavier one.

So, I read another book before returning to Kavir. Then I tried it again. If I remember correctly, I read Kavir three times. And each time, I could barely understand maybe 10-15% of it. It was just too heavy for a teenager.

Shariati's books were just a gate for me, a gate that opened other gates, and other gates. They were an eye-opening way to see the world from a different perspective, to see life in a different light. Not to limit myself to what my family or my neighborhood had to offer. At that time, there was nothing encouraged other than being religious, going to the mosque, praying five times a day, and doing these same things over and over. There weren't any opportunities to learn something new, something that could change your life, or your beliefs, or even just open your mind a little. Everything was limited, and the government was so dictatorial, just like they still are today, they banned everything: books, music, ideas. Nothing existed except Islamic content.

Shariati, a modern Muslim writer, wrote about and even criticized Muslim parents for the way they were teaching their children about Islam, and how that strictness was pushing children away from it. His books showed me that other ideas existed in this world besides Islam.

I was still a teenager, too young to truly know who I was or what I wanted to be. I didn't want to be on any "side." Sometimes I would think, my parents, my family, my neighbors are all Muslim, if I don't practice Islam, maybe a big punishment is waiting for me after death. On the other hand, I didn't want to live with that fear. I wanted something new, something that freed me from that constant pressure, something that helped me understand the world in a different way.

One thing I never understood, and still don't understand, is that religions say God is kind and forgiving, that He/She will forgive us for our mistakes. But at the same time, they scare children by saying, if you don't pray, if you don't fast during

Ramadan, God will punish you in the other world. I was confused. One day, I would become religious again, praying and fasting. The next day, I wouldn't believe in anything and would protest everything. Those were confusing moments.

But I knew one thing:

If I read more, I would understand more. If I researched and saw things from other perspectives, then deep inside myself, I would finally be able to say, Yes, this is for me, or No, this is not for me. And I would no longer have to live with fear and worry.

Of course, I didn't want to study religion or read religious books. I wanted to look at these ideas through the lens of philosophy, how philosophy viewed religion, existence, fear, and meaning. And sometimes through psychology as well. Those were going to be my next steps, a new path in my life, shaped by everything these books had opened inside me.

As I was transitioning from middle school to high school, my reading habits were transitioning with me as well. Slowly but surely, I moved from psychology and philosophy to poetry. I fell in love with poems, and I read them nonstop. Poetry became a huge part of my life, and it still is today. At that time, I memorized many poems. Today, I can barely memorize anything anymore.

Poetry aligned with everything I was searching for. It was sad, it was happy, it was deep. It forced me to go inside every sentence, every word, and think about its meaning. Poetry in Iran is very different from poetry in the Western world. Words in Persian poetry can carry many meanings at the same time. For example, the moon is a symbol of beauty. In Iran, if someone wants to say you are beautiful, they might say, "You are a moon," meaning you are gorgeous. Because of this, you see many symbolic words in poems, and each reader can interpret them in their own way.

Often, poems don't have just one meaning; they belong to the moment and to the person reading them.

When you read poems written by activists or political poets, you know that every word carries pain, sadness, and a lived experience. Instead of putting those feelings into bullets, they put them into words. They turn pain into poetry and place it inside a book. Instead of killing, they try to educate people through art. That idea touched me deeply, and that's why I love poetry so much.

I cried reading many poems. I told people I loved them with poems. I even expressed disagreement, or distance, or pain with others through poetry. In our culture, poetry is one of the strongest forms of expression, and I fell deeply into it.

That was when I discovered Ahmad Shamloo, an Iranian poet, activist, and writer. Most of his poems were political, with deep meaning hidden inside every line. Because of that, many of his books were banned in Iran. He also translated and interpreted poems from poets around the world. Through him, I read poems by Langston Hughes, an American poet, activist, and novelist. His poems were powerful and beautiful in a way that felt familiar to me, even across cultures.

At that point, I was fully immersed in poetry. Every day, I read poems by different poets. My room at my parents' house, and later my rooms when I moved to Tehran, had walls covered with pictures of Ahmad Shamloo. For me, he was the god of poetry.

And when I packed my luggage, a few of his books always made their way with me, first to Turkey, and later to the United States.

Reading those books not only changed my thought process and my perspective on life, but they also gave me something else. Something that calmed me down. Something that made me feel like I was creating, like I was doing something meaningful. I was writing.

The Price of Writing

I started writing small pieces just for myself. I would write, then tear up the pages, throw them away, burn them, whatever it took. Writing became a way to release what was inside me. Because of that, in both middle school and high school, I always received the highest grades in essay writing in school.

I will never forget the day I got into serious trouble because of one of those essays.

In high school, we were given an assignment to write about one of the Muslim prophets. Instead of writing something expected or praise-filled, I chose to write critically. That decision changed everything. They called me into the office, not the principal's office, but the assistant principal's office, the second most powerful person in the school.

He told me I should be ashamed of myself. Ashamed of my parents. Ashamed of the neighborhood I lived in. My parents' house was close to one of the biggest mosques in the city, a mosque famous for celebrating this particular prophet, and that made everything worse. What I had written became a "big deal."

He told me I was going to be suspended from high school forever. That I would never be allowed to come back. And he was going to call my parents and tell them everything.

It was one of the most terrifying moments of my life.

On the one hand, it was my first real experience of being threatened because of my writing. I was only in my first or second year of high school, and I was terrified. My stress was through the roof. My mind was racing through every possible outcome: how would my dad react? How would my mom react? What would my siblings say? Everything felt like it was collapsing.

I cried. I begged. I told him I didn't mean any harm. I said I was just asking questions, just being curious.

While I was crying and begging, my teacher walked into the office. He didn't say anything at first. He just sat there and listened. He watched me cry. He watched me beg.

Then they asked me to leave the office and wait outside, behind the door. After some time, my teacher came out and said, "I talked to him. Here's the deal."

He told me that if I wrote something positive about the prophet, brought it to class the following week, and read it out loud, the assistant principal would forgive me and would not call my parents. But for one week, I was suspended. I had to come to school, but I was not allowed to enter any classrooms. I had to sit outside, behind the doors, and listen to the lessons without participating.

I agreed.

I wrote what they wanted, even though my heart wasn't in it, because I had to protect myself. I was just a teenager. I didn't understand why questioning something, being curious, or writing critically could cause so much trouble.

But that experience taught me something important.

Writing had become my refuge. I had borrowed it from books, and especially from poetry. Poetry helped me deeply. No one in my family was a writer. Writing was something that became mine.

It became my friend.

It became my secret.

When I couldn't talk to anyone, I wrote. I put everything on paper, and when I felt calmer, I destroyed the pages. Burned them. Tore them apart. It was another path that slowly led me toward writing, and toward the life I would later live.

When Friendship Crossed Borders

Days were passing slowly, but I was falling in love with Turkey more and more. Still, somewhere deep inside, I knew this love had limits. Turkey could never be my permanent home. The country does not accept refugees as long-term residents, even though it is the largest host nation for refugees in the world. That fact alone shows how deeply hospitality, generosity, and kindness run in the hearts of Turkish people.

Back home, things were not like that. In Iran, Afghans, even though many speak the same language, rarely have opportunities. They couldn't easily become citizens, attend university, or secure good jobs. None of those paths was open to them. So, when I saw what Turkey was doing, opening its doors to people who had lost everything, I understood just how valuable that generosity was.

One afternoon, as these thoughts sat quietly in the back of my mind, I received a phone call. The number was from Kayseri, so I assumed it was my friend who visited sometimes. But when I picked up, it wasn't him. It was one of my other closest friends, someone I deeply respect for his principles, his beliefs, and his unwavering consistency.

It was Hazhir.

I was so glad to hear his voice, and I couldn't hide it. I was relieved he had finally left Iran. He had always been under watch. He had been tortured. He had been imprisoned as a teenager, just because of his political beliefs. So, when he told me he was on his way to Niğde and would stay with me until he figured out the next steps in his refugee process, I felt grateful and comforted.

Hazhir and his mother arrived a short time later. We had so much to catch up on, stories about home, about people we knew, about everything we had missed in each other's lives. Their arrival felt like a bridge connecting my old life to my new one. Back in Tehran, we had been roommates when we first moved there to continue our journalism. We worked together, became close friends, and lived together for a long time. When I left Tehran, he had stayed.

We had a wonderful time together in Niğde. His mother wasn't just his mother; she was like a friend to both of us. We laughed, went out, and showed her the city and its historical places. When she eventually left, I could tell she felt more comfortable knowing her son was safe with me.

But Hazhir's situation was far more dangerous than mine. For him, applying as a refugee was truly life-threatening. Iranian agents and spies were everywhere in Turkey, and they would not hesitate to kill him.

I knew that risk too well.

Just a few months before he arrived, I had received a threatening phone call from Iranian state agents. They told me they would kill me. I reported it to the Niğde police and to the UN. The police were incredibly supportive; they even offered me a bodyguard or someone to watch my home. But I told them no, my apartment was right behind the police station. I felt safe with them so close.

Because of all these risks, Hazhir couldn't stay long. He stayed with me for about 45 days, maybe two months, and then he left Niğde for Istanbul, and from Istanbul, he went to Germany. His new life began there, while I continued waiting for my next interview.

Yet even after he left, his presence lingered in the apartment, like a reminder of where we came from and what we had both survived.

My friendship with Hazhir goes back to when we were both teenagers. He is younger than I am, but he has always been more knowledgeable, and he has probably read as many books as you could count the hair on my head. He is also an author and a poet, and his writing style is one of the most beautiful written in Farsi.

When I was in high school, I would constantly go back and forth between being religious and not being religious. It had always been like that for me, ever since elementary school. When I started mountain climbing, I leaned toward being more non-religious. A mutual friend told me I should meet Hazhir. He said, "He's young, but very knowledgeable, and I think you'll enjoy his company." I agreed.

That moment became one of those small life decisions that ended up shaping my entire future.

In Zanjan, there were only two movie theaters, and the more famous one was called Cinema Ghods. Hazhir and I talked on the phone and agreed to meet in front of it. It was a common meeting spot for people who didn't know each other well, because you simply couldn't miss the person you were looking for. When I arrived, Hazhir was exactly as my friend had described: a tall, energetic teenager, full of enthusiasm. He immediately started talking about the books he was reading and the ideas he wanted to share. I told him honestly that I wasn't fully non-religious and that I still went back and forth.

Hazhir came prepared. He said, "I have something for you. If you read this book, maybe you'll finally make up your mind." If I'm not mistaken, the book was called Alphabet of Philosophy or something similar. I borrowed it, read it, and our friendship began.

Over time, our friendship grew even stronger. Through him, I met more people, a group of teenagers, and even though I was the oldest among them, I still felt like one of them, since I was still in high school.

When I graduated from high school, I had to serve two years of mandatory military service. While I was serving, I heard that

Hazhir had been arrested because he had written something and distributed it by throwing copies into people's yards. The government arrested him immediately.

The news hit me like a punch to the chest.

I couldn't do anything to help him, not while I was in the military. All I could do was hope, pray, and send him whatever positive energy I could. Thankfully, he was eventually released, and our friendship continued unchanged.

I once told Hazhir how interesting it was that sometimes we disagreed, sometimes even yelled at each other, but our friendship only grew stronger. I think it was because we valued the friendship more than any disagreement we had. As I mentioned earlier, I truly admire Hazhir for his consistency, his refusal to change who he is. He is the same person he was when he was a teenager. He paid the price for his beliefs and ideas, yet he always stood by them.

I grew close to Hazhir's family. We were all good friends. One funny memory I have is about their little dog, a small dog whose breed I can't remember. Once, when they went on a trip, they asked me to feed her twice a day. But she had this hilarious habit of protesting whenever they were gone. She wouldn't eat for the first day or two. On the third day, hunger would finally win, and she would eat. I became so worried, but when I called them, they said, "Don't worry, that's just how she is."

Now Hazhir is in Germany, and I am in the United States. We haven't seen each other in sixteen years. But he is one of those friends who stays permanently in your heart, no matter the distance, no matter the years.

I write about Hazhir here because these memories are tied to my time in Turkey, when he came, when he stayed with me, when he began his own journey as a refugee. Those days connected our past and our future in a way I will never forget.

He is one of the few people whose presence shaped my life, and whose friendship time could never be erased.

Between Silence and Words

Mountain climbing was one of the most meaningful activities of my life. It was where I made real friends, friends who did not compete with each other but helped each other. In the mountains, when someone fell behind, everyone stopped. When someone struggled, others jumped in. If a backpack felt too heavy, hands reached out to carry part of it. It was never about reaching the top first. It was about moving forward together, enjoying nature, and sharing each other's presence.

Mountain climbing is not easy. You carry heavy packs. Your body is under pressure. Your mind wanders. High elevation makes everything harder. In those moments, you rely on the people around you. You trust them. You know that if you stop, someone will stand next to you and help you take the next step. That trust shaped me deeply.

But the mountains were not only about physical difficulty. They were about freedom.

In the mountains, there was no fear. No Iranian intelligence unit is listening carefully to see if we crossed a line. We talked freely. We argued freely, without fear of interrogation or punishment. We could breathe.

Women were free there, too. In cities, at that time, women could not walk without a scarf to cover their heads. But in the mountains, they took it off. They lived. They laughed. They were themselves. That freedom stayed with me.

While hiking, someone with a good voice would often start singing. Soon, everyone joined. Traditional songs filled the mountains. In the evenings, after setting up our tents, we gathered around the fire. We ate together, shared what little food we had, and sang late into the night until exhaustion pulled us to sleep. Mornings began with sunrise, silence, and a sense of belonging.

Those moments shaped my life in ways I did not understand at the time.

The mountains also taught me how hardship can bring people closer. Sometimes we did not have enough water. Sometimes we barely had food. I remember one trip when a friend and I had nothing but chocolate and peanuts. One night at high elevation, we ran out of water completely. The next day, we had to walk down just to find a place where we could drink. I was falling over again and again, unable to balance myself. It was painful. It was hard. But hands reached out. Someone touched my back. Someone waited. Someone stayed with me. Even the hardest moments became meaningful because we were not alone.

One time, we traveled south to see a beautiful waterfall. Our group included people of all ages, from young children to elderly hikers. We had to take a train to reach the trailhead. It was around the Iranian New Year, and tickets were impossible to find. We had bought them far in advance. On our way back, we realized something terrible: our tickets had expired a month earlier.

I was leading the group at that time, and the responsibility crushed me. But we didn't panic. We talked. One friend said he knew someone who might help. He made a call. In the end, they let all of us sit in the train's restaurant car for the entire journey home. That moment taught me something I never forgot: problems are not solved alone. They are solved together.

Mountain climbing changed me. It changed all of us who climbed in Iran. It made us open-minded. It taught us to think differently, to rely on each other, to trust silence as much as words. And maybe that is why the government never liked it.

In ways I didn't realize back then, mountain climbing even led me toward journalism. Through those trips, I started writing sports news and small articles for a weekly paper in Zanjan called

Sedaye Zanjan, The Voice of Zanjan. It was another path opening quietly, shaped by the same values I learned in the mountains: honesty, responsibility, and standing with others.

I could have never imagined that The Voice of Zanjan would open a door that would change my life forever.

At The Voice of Zanjan, we didn't receive any formal training. I didn't know journalistic standards, ethics, or rules. I was simply writing, not knowing whether what I was doing was right or wrong, because no one had taught me what "right" even meant in journalism. I was learning by doing.

Then another door opened.

For the first time in Zanjan, a daily newspaper announced it was hiring. Until then, we only had weekly papers. Seeing those advertisements on the streets felt unreal. The paper was called Mardome No, New People. I applied, attended the interview, and they offered me a position. But there was a condition: I would have to complete six months of unpaid training.

I accepted without hesitation.

It was my dream. I wanted to become a journalist, maybe even a writer. And ultimately, I paid a high price for that decision. I left a good-paying job. I spent all my savings during those first six months. Still, journalism is something I have never regretted pursuing. Not for a single moment. It became another essential path in my life, one that shaped me in the way I had always hoped my life would be shaped.

Slowly, that small group of journalists, mostly young, inexperienced people like me, guided by editors who had years of experience, became something more than colleagues. We became friends. Real friends. It felt exactly like mountain climbing. No competition. No hesitation. We helped each other grow, improve, and become better journalists. And sometimes, we helped each other survive financially.

Most days, we brought food from home. Once or twice a month, we collected whatever money we had and bought lunch together, nothing fancy, usually fast food. There was a famous place in Zanjan called Mehdi's Sandwich. At that time, they made only one kind of sandwich, and they made it well. There was always a long line. Sometimes we didn't have enough money for everyone, so we put everything we had together and made sure no one was left out. That's how it worked. That's how we lived.

At the same time, another weekly newspaper was born, Moje Bidari (Wave of Awakening). It became more than a workplace. It became home.

It was just my friend Hazhir, another friend, and me, three journalists, working along with three editors. That was it. But the owner gave us something rare: freedom. We were allowed to write what we believed in. Because of that, Wave of Awakening became our heart, our responsibility, and our identity.

We were careful not to harm New People. We chose a completely different path for the weekly, because some of us were working for both publications. There were lines we couldn't cross at the daily. At the Wave of Awakening, we could push further. We practiced real journalism, interviews, reports, investigations, stories that mattered.

When we prepared our very first issue, Hazhir, another friend, and I didn't sleep for three nights. We were excited beyond words. We prepared everything ourselves. We sat with the designer, explaining how we wanted each page to look. Sometimes they were exhausted, and we kept saying, "Just one more page. Just one more." We pushed ourselves to the limit.

We didn't even go home to eat.

My house was only fifteen minutes away on foot. So were theirs. But we were afraid that if we left, even for a moment, something would go wrong. So, we stayed. We worked. We survived on one remaining pack of cigarettes and excitement alone. We wanted to reach the finish line.

When the issue finally came out, one of our editors brought his car. We filled the seats and the trunk with newspapers and distributed them ourselves. We couldn't afford to hire anyone.

Later that afternoon, another editor, who lived in Tehran, came to the office. He looked at the three of us and said, "Why do you look like this? Why are you so pale? Are you sick?"

One of us answered honestly: "We haven't eaten for three days."

He immediately called someone and ordered food. When the sandwiches arrived, maybe eighteen of them, he ate one or two. The rest disappeared in seconds.

I don't regret a single minute of my journalism life in Zanjan. Not one. Tehran was different, bigger, heavier, more complex. But in Zanjan, we gave everything we had. Our time. Our energy. Our hearts. And all of that led me to the capital, to working for the biggest newspapers and news agencies in Iran.

Under Watch

While I was in the military, I spent almost two years in Tehran. Our military unit was located in the middle of the city, very close to Enghelab Square (Revolution Square), an area famous for its bookstores and street bookstalls. People would spread books right on the sidewalks and sell them openly. Some of those books were banned in Iran.

Building trust with those sellers was not easy. You couldn't just walk up and ask for forbidden books. You had to go slowly. I started by buying regular books, books that were allowed, just to show that I wasn't a spy or connected to the government. Over time, I built a relationship with one of the sellers. I bought two or three books by Ahmad Shamlou from him.

Eventually, I asked him if he could bring me one specific book by Shamlou, Madayeh-e Bi-Seleh, Hymns Without Reward. The book was banned at that time. He said yes. When I got the book, I hid it in my drawer at the military unit, the same drawer where I kept hygiene items like toothpaste, toothbrushes, towels, things like that. Somehow, someone reported me.

Members of the military intelligence unit came and asked me to open the drawer. I was terrified. I turned red, started sweating, and couldn't stop shaking. When I opened it, they saw the books.

They said, "You read Shamlou? You should be ashamed. He is against the Islamic Revolution. He is an atheist. A communist." They took the books and took me to the military intelligence unit.

I was extremely anxious. I didn't know what to say. Then, suddenly, something came to my mind. I knew that if I wanted to get out of this, I had to say something; otherwise, I was in serious trouble.

I told them that Shamlou also had a book of love poems written for his wife, Aida, a book called Aida in the Mirror. I said those were just love poems, and that was why I bought his books.

I told them I didn't know anything about politics, atheism, or communism.

Because I mentioned that book, their tone changed. They started talking softly. "My son," they said. "Some people make mistakes. Don't read these books. They are against the Islamic Revolution." They repeated the same warnings again and again.

They took the books and let me go.

Toward the end of my military service, they made things difficult for me again. I don't know exactly why. But finally, when I finished my term of service, I was allowed to leave.

That reminds me of another incident.

It was Ramadan. We were sitting in the office. All my friends were fasting. I was the only one who was not. The windows were covered with newspapers, but we weren't allowed to cover them completely. We had to leave a strip open at the top.

While we were waiting for the time to break the fast, I started drinking tea. Suddenly, we noticed someone watching us through the uncovered part of the window. We thought it was one of our friends.

Five minutes later, we received a call from the military intelligence unit. They said whoever was drinking tea before the official time had to report to them.

My friends stood by me. They said no one had done anything wrong. The officers threatened us. If that person didn't come forward, they said, all of us would be sent to military prison.

They did exactly that.

Five of us spent three days in a military prison.

After that, when it was time to get food, we had to stand in line with a large metal pan. Our heads were shaved. We had to give the food distributor our names. Eventually, people knew our story. When we went forward, we would say, "This is for the five prisoners." And that's how we got our dinner.

All of that, prison, punishment, fear, for drinking tea, for reading a book, for thinking differently.

That was life in Iran. People were forced to live with two personalities: one at home, and one outside. No one should lose their freedom, or their life, for reading, not fasting, or believing differently from the government. Yet that fear followed us everywhere.

The Weight of Waiting

Life kept moving, working, routine, waiting. Then one night, the ASAM agent called me.

"Hamid, I have bad news," he said. "Majid's case was denied. He is very young, and I cannot bring myself to tell him. Can you give him the news?"

I agreed.

That evening, after work, Majid came to our home. My roommate and I had dinner with him, and afterward, I asked him to take a walk with me. We went to the historical hilltop area in Niğde, where there was an old stone building that had been turned into a coffee shop. We always enjoyed sitting there together, drinking tea and talking.

As we walked, I tried to gently prepare him for what I was about to say. Finally, I told him the truth. The only promise I could make was:

"When I am settled, if you ever need help with anything, I will try my best to help you."

That was truly all I could offer. I told him he could appeal the decision, but that the process was long and exhausting.

He took the news realistically. He was upset and disappointed, as anyone would be, but he did not explode or break down. I was relieved he could manage his emotions. It made the burden feel slightly lighter.

A few weeks later, I received another call from the UN. They invited me to an interview to choose my resettlement country. Once again, it was time to stay at Davut's home and prepare myself.

At the interview, my Turkish was good enough that I could speak without the interpreter. The interpreter was supposed to translate from Farsi to Turkish. The interviewer asked me whether I had a preference for a country to resettle in.

I explained that most of my politically active friends were in Germany and that I would like to go there, if possible.

But the interpreter didn't translate my answer. Instead, he yelled at me. In Iranian culture, we have a saying that means, "This is not your aunt's house where you can do whatever you want." His tone was meant to put me in my place, as if I had no right to an opinion.

I got upset. I told the interviewer that he wasn't translating my words. She asked if I felt comfortable speaking directly to her. I said yes.

I explained my preference again. She smiled politely and told me it wasn't possible. Germany had accepted many immigrants who arrived there directly, so it didn't take refugees through the UN process anymore.

"Okay," I said. "Then I have no one anywhere. Wherever you think I should go, I will go."

She explained that only three countries were accepting UN-referred refugees at that time: Canada, Australia, and the United States. Then she added, "I think the United States is the best fit for you."

I agreed immediately. I didn't know much about the other two countries. Like many people around the world, all I knew was that the United States was the land of dreams. Maybe, just maybe, one of those dreams could come true for me.

After the interview, life in Turkey continued. Time felt slow, yet full, and I found myself falling more and more in love with the country.

Turkey gave us safety, dignity, and a temporary home when we had nowhere else to go. But I knew I couldn't stay forever.

During this long period of waiting, life brought moments of calm and moments of chaos. Some nights were simple dinners with my roommate, long walks, and talking about the future. Other nights were full of visitors. Friends from Zanjan came to see me, and sometimes a close friend from Hamadan would arrive too.

Whenever I had guests, we often took a trip to Mersin, a beautiful coastal city. The sea was our escape, a place to forget, even briefly, that we were refugees waiting for paperwork to move our lives forward.

One time, we rented an apartment there. Only after getting ready for bed did we realize how filthy the sheets and blankets were. But we laughed and said, "Come on... It's refugee life. Let it go."

That kind of humor was how we survived.

After returning to Niğde from one of those trips, I got extremely sick. My entire body itched terribly, yet there were no marks, no rash, no bites, nothing. A couple of friends took care of me, took me to the hospital, and after a few days of medication, the itching finally disappeared. But the experience reminded me again how fragile life as a refugee could be. Even illness felt heavier when you were alone in a foreign country.

But thank I had two really good friends, one Iranian and one Turkish. My Iranian friend took me to his home and hosted me for several days. He took care of everything: he prepared breakfast, lunch, and dinner, and didn't let me do a single thing. I was just resting while he handled everything for me. I had to shower twice a day because of the medication the hospital gave me, and each time I showered, I had to change all my clothes. He helped me with everything, and having him by my side made those days so much easier.

On the other hand, Mehmet, who is another amazing friend, helped me just as much. Even after I left Turkey, he was always there for me whenever I needed to talk or vent. Back then, even though he was a student, and life wasn't easy for him financially, and even though his roommates might not have been thrilled about it, he still came every single day, picked up my clothes, took them home, washed and dried them, and brought them back to me. It meant so much to have such good friends supporting me through that illness.

Then came a night I will never forget, New Year's Eve.

My friends and I went out for dinner. While we were walking to the restaurant from my home, I didn't feel cold or even a chill, nothing at all. Even though it was snowy and freezing, I was completely comfortable with the weather, and because of that, I only wore a regular jacket. Inside the restaurant, I felt perfectly warm, but Niğde's winters were harsh, and when we stepped outside, within two minutes, the cold hit me so deeply that I couldn't stop shaking. My friends piled their jackets, scarves, and hats on me, but I still shivered uncontrollably. We hurried home, played music, laughed, danced, and welcomed the new year together.

It turned into a beautiful night despite the cold, one of those nights that felt like a small reminder that joy was still possible, even in difficult circumstances.

Life kept going, waiting for updates, working long hours, learning to survive in a place that was both kind and temporary. Through all of it, I tried to stay strong. I didn't know what the next chapter would bring, but I knew one thing:

Every step forward was a step closer to the life I hoped for.

Twelve Hours to a New Future

Life returned to normal. Then I got the call: my first U.S. interview.

Now I had to make another trip, another long trip. This time, I needed to go to Istanbul instead of Ankara, because all U.S. interviews were held there. As always, I was on the bus, and I couldn't sleep. All I did was think, think about possibilities, about the past, about the future. I never understood when people said, "Don't think about the past," or "Don't think about the future, just be in the present." That has never been me. I can't do that. I think about everything. I want to acknowledge my mistakes and the things I regret so I don't repeat them. And I always want to think about the future and have a plan. To me, it feels impossible to just live in the present without thinking ahead.

So, for the entire twelve hours from Niğde to Istanbul, I thought and thought. And to be honest, sometimes I cried, cried for the things I missed the most. In Zanjan, for example, there was a mountain we always climbed on Fridays. Friday is the only weekend in Iran. The mountain is called Gavazang, and from there we continued to another mountain called Amand. We would go early in the morning, have breakfast, make tea on a small fire, and enjoy time with friends. Sometimes my friends would climb the difficult rock walls of Amand. I never did, because it was extremely hard, but I loved sitting there watching them. Afterward, we shared lunch like a potluck, with everyone putting their food on the ground, and whoever wanted could eat whatever they liked.

I missed those moments deeply. I knew I would miss Gavazang forever. Even today, it is still the only geographic place in Iran that I miss with all my heart.

Eventually, we arrived at the bus station. I had booked a hotel for one night so I could rest and be ready for my interview the next day. When morning came, I was nervous, naturally nervous, because so many things were unknown. I didn't know what questions they would ask, who would interview me, or what the atmosphere would be like. Because of that anxiety, I didn't use the bus or metro. I was afraid of getting lost, so I took a taxi instead.

The taxi driver was from the Kurdish region of Turkey, and we started chatting. During that short ride, he shared with me one of the most beautiful philosophical things I've ever heard. I asked him about the conflicts between Kurds and Turks, and he said, "Brother, it's not the people who fight each other. We Kurds have daughters who marry Turkish men, and Turks have daughters who marry Kurdish men or vice versa. It's the governments, the power, and the money that put people in front of each other to fight. Not the people."

It was so deep that it made me think even more. Later in life, I realized how true it was. For example, Iran and Iraq were at war for years, but later I found wonderful Iraqi friends.

We talked about everything until we reached the location. It wasn't at the embassy, but at a U.S. immigration office in Istanbul. When I arrived, they guided us to the waiting area, a basement full of people and very uncomfortable chairs. There were no windows, as far as I remember. It was dark, extremely warm, and crowded. We weren't given a specific interview time; we were only told to be there around 7 or 8 a.m. I arrived around 7 and waited for hours. Waiting has always been my biggest weakness. I get anxious, and there is nothing I can do about it. I had no choice. I waited and waited until, finally, after four or five hours, they called my name.

I went into the interview room. The questions were simple: basic demographic information, why I applied for refugee status, and what military branch I served in.[3]

After the interview, I returned to Niğde and continued waiting for the main interview.

And slowly, all the exhaustion of the past year began to weigh heavily on me.

I was getting so tired of all these trips. It had been about a year since I first arrived in Turkey, and in that one year, I had already traveled countless times for interviews, paperwork, and documents. I had no choice; of course, I had to keep going, keep pushing, keep facing every difficulty in the hope of a brighter future. But still, the trips wore me down.

It was always twelve hours on a bus.

Twelve hours of not sleeping.

Twelve hours of thinking, remembering, worrying, hoping.

At the same time, those long road trips became part of my life, memories of their own. Almost every time, the person sitting next to me would start a conversation. And the moment I opened my mouth, they recognized my accent. They always smiled, always welcomed the conversation, always asked questions about Iran, life there, culture, food, everything. I never had a bad experience. They were never defensive or hostile. In fact, they loved it. They admired how quickly I had learned Turkish and how well I could communicate. They were proud of me as if I belonged to them.

They always said the same thing:

"We are brothers."

Or if it was a woman:

---

[3] In Iran, all men must serve for two years. Women, even if they want to, are forbidden from serving.

"We are brothers and sisters."

Those words made me happy every time.

One interesting thing I learned later: in many Western countries, people say that if you display your national flag everywhere, on your house, on your car, it can be seen as a sign of nationalism or racism. But in Turkey, the flag is everywhere. Every city. Every street. Every neighborhood. Turkish flags wave from balconies, shops, cars, schools, everywhere. And still, Turkish people are not racist. Not at all. They simply love their country and respect their flag. Of course, like anywhere in the world, not 100% of people are the same. But in general, Turks are warm, kind, and welcoming. Maybe that's why they are the top host country for refugees in the entire world.

Those long road trips continued. Then, I was extremely social, not like today. I would make friends within seconds. Sometimes we exchanged numbers, sometimes we invited each other to try dishes from our cultures. These strangers became memories of their own.

One time, when I returned to Niğde, a group of Turkish university students, none of them originally from Niğde, invited a couple of my friends and me for dinner. They were all friends of Mehmet, who became one of my closest friends in Turkey. The way we met was simple: Turkey has a celebration they call something like "Young People's Week," when popular singers give free concerts at universities, and anyone can attend. For one whole week in Niğde, there were concerts every night, and of course, we went. That's where we met Mehmet and some of the others.

And that same week…

I fell in love with my Turkish girlfriend.

Dinner with Mehmet and his friends was one of the most beautiful nights I ever had in Turkey. They were wonderful hosts. They respected us deeply because we were older, and in both Iran and Turkey, respecting elders is a cultural value. We laughed, ate delicious food, shared stories, and created memories that stayed with me forever.

Those friendships, those nights, those small moments of kindness, they helped me survive the waiting.

Eventually, a friend called to tell me that an Iranian journalist, a woman whose name I knew but had never met, had been assigned to Niğde by the U.N. They asked if she could be my roommate, since my current roommate had already been approved for the U.S. and had a travel date. I agreed.

At the same time, my landlord told me he needed the apartment back because he was returning to Niğde. So, I began searching for a new place.

And life continued, one step at a time, one interview at a time, one hope at a time.

Neighbors, Nights, and New Roots

I had to leave my apartment, the apartment I truly loved, the place where I made so many memories with my family, my friends, and everyone who came to visit. Even though sometimes my roommate gave me a hard time, we still created beautiful memories there. And now, I had to pack it all up and leave.

One of the funniest memories from that apartment happened thanks to ASAM, the organization I mentioned earlier that supported refugees. They provided refugees with charcoal for the winter, since the heating system relied mainly on charcoal, and using electricity or gas was far too expensive. One day, a huge truck arrived with what must have been around a thousand kilograms of charcoal, packed in heavy bags, maybe fifty kilos each, maybe a little less. We had to carry all of those bags up to the fifth floor. It took forever, and we were exhausted, but it also became one of those ridiculous memories that you laugh about later.

The very first time we tried to burn the charcoal in the heater, we had no idea what we were doing. We nearly burned the entire place down. Other times, it simply refused to burn. It took us days, maybe weeks, to finally get the hang of it. But once we did, we actually loved it. We would put potatoes on top of the heater, letting them roast slowly until they were cooked and crispy. Sometimes we ate them plain, sometimes with drinks, always laughing.

Leaving that apartment wasn't just leaving a place; it was leaving a chapter of my life. I packed those memories into my heart and moved on, but even now, I can see that apartment clearly. It was one of the places where I made the best memories of my entire life, and I will never forget it.

Finally, I found a building made up of two small complexes, three apartments in each. In one building lived a family: the parents and their two adult sons. In the second building, where I rented the top floor, two apartments were occupied by Turkish students. It was the only building in the entire area, standing alone, and my journalist friend, being a single woman, didn't like the idea of possibly living alone there in the future. But it was what it was.

The landlords were wonderful. When I wasn't working, they'd sometimes stop by to chat and drink tea. They loved the cube sugar I had brought from Iran. In their backyard, they had a fire pit where, every year, the whole family gathered to make huge pots of homemade tomato paste. They always shared a small container of it with us.

To reach the police station from this building, we walked for about forty minutes. But it was a pleasant walk, so we didn't mind. We only used public transportation when we were exhausted or carrying heavy groceries. Other than that, we walked everywhere, because in that isolated area, the bus stop was far, and it was just easier to walk.

And so life went on quietly and patiently, as I continued waiting for the interview that would decide my future.

One day, a friend called to tell me that a family of three had just arrived in Niğde. They were relatives of one of my former editors from Tehran. The family was struggling to find a place to rent, and my friend asked if I could help. I went to meet them, and the moment I saw them, I could tell how scared they were. They explained they had converted to Christianity and feared Turkish landlords would refuse to rent to them. They felt they needed to confess their religion to every landlord so no one would accuse them of hiding anything.

I remembered a Turkish man I knew, someone who, at one point, I believe had even served as the mayor of the city. He had always been kind to refugees and often invited Iranians to spend time at his small farm. So, I called him and explained the situation.

"Where are you?" he asked.

I gave him the address. Within minutes, he arrived, picked us up, and said he had an apartment they could rent.

He drove us to the unit, a modern and very clean place. The family immediately loved it. But they were still anxious and begged me to tell him the truth about their religion before agreeing to anything. So, I pulled him aside and explained that the family was Christian and wanted to be upfront about it.

He looked at me with genuine surprise and said something so simple yet so powerful that it stunned all of us:

"Your religion is yours. It has nothing to do with me."

The family was shocked. They had been told that Turkish people disliked Christians, but at that moment, they realized how wrong those assumptions were. Just like anywhere in the world, there are all kinds of people, and kindness exists everywhere, too.

Their little girl, full of sweetness and energy, kept asking if this was really going to be their new home. When the landlord agreed, they were overjoyed. Seeing them so relieved made the entire moment unforgettable.

Around the same time, I received another call from the U.S. Embassy for my second interview. I was thrilled, thinking this would be the final step. Later, I learned that this was not the end at all. After the interview, the background check would begin, and that could take months.

I took the bus to Istanbul once again. The interview this time was extremely difficult. The officers were incredibly knowledgeable about Iran, especially its military structure. They asked detailed questions: where I served, my exact role, how long, what responsibilities I had, everything. They seemed to know every branch and every region inside Iran.

I'm not completely certain, but it felt like they had my entire U.N. file in front of them. They repeated some of the exact questions from my U.N. interview, checking for consistency. The interview lasted four or five hours with interpreters.

A few weeks later, I was notified that the United States had accepted my case. The relief was indescribable, but they reminded me that now the background check would begin, and that it could take time.

Most people who interviewed around the same time as I did had already flown to their new countries, but I was still waiting. I had no idea why mine was delayed until a Turkish journalist friend told me his theory: my last name. The president of Iran at the time also had "Nezhad" in his name.

He said, "Because of that, they'll probably do extra checks to make sure you're not a government agent or spy."

That possibility never occurred to me. I realized there was still a chance they could deny my background check, and if that happened, I would have to start over, choose another country, and repeat the entire process. Though I was told that most countries require only one interview, the thought of beginning from square one was terrifying.

So, I waited, hoping the background check would eventually clear and that I wouldn't have to start the process all over again.

Niğde is such a small city that most people know each other, and because I had learned Turkish, my Iranian friends often asked me to go with them as a translator. Over time, many of the restaurants, boutiques, and little shops began to recognize me. They even knew me by name. Slowly, we all became friends. Life there had a calm rhythm, especially since the whole city seemed to revolve around one main street. On days when I wasn't working, I would walk up and down that street several times, sometimes with friends, sometimes alone.

We always tried to eat in the cheaper restaurants because that was what our budgets allowed, but even the inexpensive places served delicious food. Turkey's food culture is something special; even the simplest meals taste good.

One of my favorite things in Turkey, especially in Niğde, was the farmers' market. They had huge markets that rotated around the city, one neighborhood each day of the week. The biggest one was on Thursdays, not far from where I lived. You could find everything: fruits, vegetables, clothes, shoes, pajamas, underwear, anything you could imagine. And the produce in Turkey was unbelievable. I still don't think you can find fruits and vegetables like that anywhere else in the world. I knew I would miss it someday.

But at the same time, I didn't fully know if I would miss it or not, because I had no real understanding of what the United States was like. Everything I "knew" was only from what friends told me. I didn't watch Western movies or listen to Western music, so I had no picture of American life in my mind. That uncertainty scared me. I kept thinking: I'm already thirty-three. Learning a new language, adapting to a new culture, starting from zero, it's going to be so hard.

But I also knew something else about myself: I'm tough, no matter how hard it would be, I knew I would learn the language, adapt to the culture, work hard, and eventually fit into my new life. That was the promise I kept repeating to myself.

I was going to miss many things: my old friends from Iran, the new friends I made in Turkey, the routines, the food, and the familiarity. One of my friends once told me something that I will never forget:

"Immigration is an F..ed-up process. First, you build memories for decades in your home country. Then you go to a second country and build more memories for one, two, five, or even ten years. Then you leave again and start over in a third country. It's really messed up."

He was right. But sometimes life doesn't give you many choices. Sometimes the choices come down to survival.

I had a choice: I could stay in Iran, lose my young life, or even die… or I could leave everything behind and try to stay alive. I chose life. I chose the road that gave me hope. And once I chose it, I knew I had to accept whatever came next and adapt to every new challenge.

In the Waiting Room of Tomorrow

In addition to the lengthy background check, as a refugee bound for the United States, a full medical exam was also required. I was told that if you have certain illnesses, the U.S. might not allow you to enter. I'm not entirely sure which illnesses those are, but I believe there are only a few specific ones. When you receive a date for your medical exam, it's usually good news; it means your background check has likely passed, and you are getting closer to your departure date.

I received a call from the U.S. Embassy with the date for my medical exam, which was to take place at their hospital in Istanbul, a place called AMERİKAN HASTANESİ (the Hospital of America).

This meant I had to take another trip to Istanbul for the medical exam, another long journey, twelve hours on the bus each way, twenty-four hours round-trip. I bought my ticket and made my way toward Istanbul once again. My brain wouldn't turn off like it does whenever I am on the road. I knew that I was finally moving toward my final destination. I didn't know for sure, but I assumed I would have a much better life ahead of me. I knew how far I was moving from my family, my friends, my culture, the food I loved, and everything familiar. That part was painful. I didn't know what to do with those feelings, but this was the path I had chosen, and I wanted to continue. I wanted to fight through my thoughts and the duality of feelings inside me. It was difficult, but I had to do it.

One thing I was truly thankful for was my patience. Many people always tell me how patient I am, and I think I inherited that from my mother. I am patient, until I'm not. When I lose that patience, I lose it badly, and without thinking about the consequences. But on this journey, I didn't want to lose anything, not my patience, and not my hope. I wanted to keep moving to see where the next step would take me, and what my new life might look like. There was always a big question mark in my mind: What does life look like on the other side of the world? That question reminded me of when I was in middle school and suffered with epilepsy. Now, on my way to Istanbul, all those memories rushed back and refused to leave me alone.

When I finally arrived, I went straight to Amerikan Hastanesi, the Hospital of America. It was a very modern, clean, and organized hospital. Everyone was polite and patient. Even though I had been healthy all my life, aside from the epilepsy, I was nervous. We were told that having some illnesses could prevent us from entering the United States. So of course I worried: What if I had something I didn't know about? What if my lab results showed something? What if? What if? what if?...

Eventually, they called my name. I went through the full medical examination from the top of my head to the bottom of my feet. I had never experienced such an extensive exam in my life. When it was over, they told me they would report the results directly to the U.S. immigration office. As far as I remember, they didn't give us the results themselves.

After the exam, I made my way home again, exhausted in every possible way, and that was when the nuisances slowly started to appear.

Since the medical exam meant that I was getting closer to leaving Turkey, my journalist friend was a little worried, as she was living alone in the apartment with no other buildings nearby. We started searching for another apartment for her together. One of my Turkish friends, who is still a good friend to me, helped us. We walked through alleys and streets, checking phone numbers on doors and calling landlords.

Finally, a very sweet elderly woman invited us to come to her home in the afternoon when her son was home. When we arrived, her son, a university professor, greeted us. From my accent, he realized I wasn't Turkish. As Iranian Azeris, many of us consider ourselves Turks, although we speak Azeri, which is close to Turkish. I told him I was an Iranian Turk. He apologized, saying that his mother had thought we were Turkish, and she didn't want to rent to Iranians because the building was very quiet. One apartment was hers, another belonged to a single professor, and the third to a married couple. He explained that Iranians often hold loud parties until midnight, and his mother couldn't handle that.

I asked, "What if we promise it won't happen?"

"No, I'm sorry," he said.

We were about to leave, standing at the door during sunset, when he called out, "Hamid, come back. You are so sweet. I cannot say no to you." I was thrilled; it felt like a huge compliment. We went back in, discussed the rent, and finalized everything.

I knew I wouldn't be there long, as I had already completed my medical exam, and she would stay until her U.N. case was approved.

The next morning, when I went to buy bread for breakfast, I found a bag hanging on the door handle. Inside were two pieces of bread and a pack of cigarettes, our new landlord's way of helping us start our day. Later, the sweet elderly woman brought us lunch, saying, "You must be tired and exhausted from moving. I wanted you to have this." This continued for several days. Eventually, we realized that if she kept doing this daily, the cost of the bread and cigarettes alone would exceed our rent. We insisted she stop, but she continued occasionally anyway.

While we were living in that apartment, we kept every promise we had made to the landlord and her son. We were quiet, we didn't have anyone over, and we never made noise after 10 p.m. If we wanted to smoke, we always went outside. We were extremely mindful, because we wanted them to know how grateful we were for their hospitality and for trusting us. I truly wish I still had a connection with them, but I don't. The only reason I don't is that I'm ashamed.

After I left Turkey, my journalist friend, who had replaced me in the apartment, brought four or five more people, other journalists from Iran, to live with her. One day, I received a call from the landlord's son. Even then, he was still so polite and patient. He didn't say anything like, "You promised," or "You told us this wouldn't happen." He simply explained the situation kindly: they were loud, awake all night, talking and playing music, and not considering that the entire complex was quiet and peaceful.

I cannot describe how ashamed I was. I was sweating, I turned red, and the only words I could say were, "I'm so sorry. I'm so sorry." But deep inside, I knew that my apology couldn't change anything anymore. I couldn't believe how someone could disrespect that sweet elderly woman, someone who treated her almost like a daughter.

I was angry, really angry. When I lose my patience, I lose it badly, and that moment was one of them. I called my journalist friend immediately. All of them were together in the apartment when I called. And I told her, "Listen, the only reason you're in that apartment is that the landlord trusted me, and I promised none of those things would ever happen. If I get one more call from them, I will ask them to evict you."

It was the only thing I could think of. I wanted them to understand how important it was to be mindful. We were refugees in their country. We were not working. We were not the ones waking up early every morning to go to our jobs. Turkish people had responsibilities, routines, and lives. They needed rest. They needed peace. We couldn't be selfish, having late-night gatherings, loud conversations, music, and laughter while they were trying to sleep.

When I lived there, we never did any of that. Even if we stayed up late, it was behind our laptops, writing, chatting, or reading quietly. Never disturb anyone.

To this day, I still feel ashamed when I think about calling the landlord. I still cannot bring myself to do it. I don't know if anything changed after I talked to them, but I never received another call. The landlord, the way I did, so sweet, patient, and kind, I'm sure that even if they still had issues, they wouldn't call me to complain again. That's just the kind of people they were.

Finally, I received a call confirming my next important date: January 14, 2010.

The Bridge I Built in The Night

It was that time, I had to pack. Packing my belongings was never the problem. What hurt was packing my memories once more. Memories I had made in this small city, Niğde. Memories that were mostly good, though there were a few difficult ones too. But overall, Niğde had given me some of the best moments of my life.

Now I had to leave those memories behind and carry them only in my heart and my mind. Just like the memories I had already packed away from Zanjan, from Iran, my true home. And now, once again, I had to pack the memories I made with my roommates, with the friends I met here, even with the police officers who became part of my daily routine. I had to pack the memories I made on Niğde's Anne Caddesi (main street), the cute little shops, the restaurants, and the simple routines that became part of my life. I had to pack the memories from the farmers' market, the place I loved the most. The memories of my family visiting me. The memories of friends who came to see me.

How can I fit all of that into a suitcase? Into two suitcases? Even into ten or twenty? You can't. They only fit in your heart and in your mind. And it hurts deeply.

Honestly, sometimes I feel like it's all so unfair. Why is this world built in a way that some people always have to live in fear, and some people never even worry about openly criticizing their government or politicians? Why do some people carry the weight of survival every day, while others live freely without thinking twice? Life aside, even memories don't feel fair. Breaking the bridge behind you and knowing you can't return home, can't see your family, your friends, places where your heart lives, it's just not right. It's not fair.

The closer I got to the date of my flight to the United States, the stranger my emotions became. I knew it would be almost impossible for my family or friends to come visit me there. I knew it was impossible for me to go back to Iran, not unless a regime change happened. All of these thoughts made my heart race, and my anxiety spiked. Sometimes I felt like I was on the edge of a panic attack. My heart hurt so badly, I cried like a child. And the worst part was, I couldn't even tell whether the crying came from joy or from pain.

I knew my life wasn't going to be hanging in uncertainty anymore. I was finally going to a "final destination," a place where I could build a future, find a job, have a home, and stop worrying about basic survival. But I also knew I would miss everything, every single thing, and every single memory I had made.

Turkey was still close to Iran. Whenever my family wanted to visit, it wasn't a big deal for them. But now... now I was going to be thousands and thousands of miles away from everything I loved.

I didn't know what to think. One minute, I was joyful, jumping around, excited, and celebrating. The next minute, I was deep inside my own soul, thinking about everything I was leaving behind. And the truth is, I hate the unknown. I really do. And this next step was nothing but a series of unknowns.

I didn't know what life looked like over there.

I didn't know what people looked like over there or how they would treat me.

I didn't know how long it would take to learn the language.

I didn't know if I would be able to find a job.

I didn't know when, or if, I would ever see my family again.

I didn't even know how long the flight would be or what would happen when I landed.

The only thing I knew was the city I would be resettled in, and that was only because of Hazhir. He had a political activist friend in the U.S., Dr. Masali, who agreed to be my sponsor. That was it, the only piece of information I had. I didn't know Dr. Masali personally. I only knew his name.

Sometimes I told myself I wished I wouldn't leave, even if staying in Iran cost me my life. Sometimes I was grateful that I had made this choice. The dual feelings were overwhelming: joy mixed with fear, hope mixed with heartbreak. Every immigrant understands this conflict. When you leave a country without the possibility of returning, the emotional cost is enormous.

Bringing my family to America... that would be almost impossible. Thinking about all that drove me crazy. I kept going back and forth with myself. One minute I cried, the next minute I laughed. One minute, I relived every memory from my childhood through age 31 in Iran, then ages 31 to 33 in Turkey... and now, at age 33, I was preparing to be born again.

Immigration is a rebirth.

You start everything from zero.

A new language.

A new culture.

New food.

New jobs.

New everything.

I asked myself over and over: Am I ready for this?

I thought of every person in my life for the past 33 years. My mother was always there in my mind. I wished that the last picture I had of my father wasn't that heartbreaking moment in Istanbul, when he hugged me so tightly and cried so loudly. That image still hurts me. I didn't know when I would see my beautiful family again. My nieces, who would probably be grown up by the time I saw them next. My sisters, the angels of my life. My nephews. My brothers-in-law. And my sweet, kind, generous brother. I missed him so much. I wish he had come to Turkey so I could have seen him one last time.

I never thought, truly never thought, that it would be this hard. I always imagined that once I left Iran, everything would be joyful. But I was wrong. Every step was difficult. Even though most of my memories in Turkey were good, the journey itself was hard. I lost many things to gain what I gained. And I knew the next step would be the same: I would lose more to gain something new.

Sometimes, I couldn't help but think: How unfair life can be.

Now that I have had my departure date, I have stopped working. But I wish I had never stopped. When I was working, it kept me distracted. I could just focus on the job. But the moment I wasn't working, my brain refused to stop for even a second. It kicked me out of the present and dragged me back, back to my life, back to my childhood, to my teenage years, to my adult life… thirty-one years in Iran and eighteen months in Turkey. My mind wouldn't stop replaying memories for even a moment.

Now I was going all the way back, returning to memories I had buried for years. My entire childhood was destroyed by two things. First, sickness. My legs always hurt, and eventually we found out I was suffering from rheumatism. It took years of medication throughout my childhood until I finally got better. And second, the eight-year war between Iran and Iraq. That war destroyed my entire childhood. I lived in constant fear, fear of bombs falling, fear of dying, fear that my family or friends might die. I am certain it was the same for my Iraqi brothers and sisters. That's what war does. It destroys the lives of innocent people on both sides.

It was impossible not to think about the role of the Western world in the constant wars in the Middle East. So many people blame Middle Easterners for "not fighting for their freedom," or say, "there is never peace in the Middle East." But that is not the truth. Not even close. For decades, Western governments have helped install and support dictatorships in the region, dictators who silence their people and crush protests with violence. When people demand freedom, their own governments kill them, while the powerful nations that put those governments in place keep benefiting from money, oil, and control. These are political games, and regular people have no place in the game except as casualties. War is a game of money and power, played by a few, paid for by millions.

My childhood was destroyed because of powerful people playing with innocent lives. I always lived in fear, and so did everyone my age, and surely every Iraqi child my age as well. It didn't matter where we were, at home, playing outside, or sitting in a classroom; we had to stay alert at all times. The moment the siren went off, we had to run. Run fast, to a basement or any spot that might protect us from the bombs coming down.

And it wasn't only Iraq bombing Iran. I am sure Iran did the same to Iraq. Both governments destroyed countless children's lives, children losing siblings, friends, parents, and cousins. Parents are losing their children in the most painful ways. For what? For money, for power, for politics.

Never, not once in history, has war been an answer to anything except greed. I still can't understand how politicians can be so selfish that they take innocent lives for their own benefit.

I remember it clearly, the day my brother was allowed to come home for just a few days while serving his mandatory military service. When he came home for a short break, my aunt invited us for lunch at her house. We began getting ready to go. She lived a little far from us, not too far, maybe fifteen to twenty minutes by car.

Just as we were about to leave, the alarms went off in my city. At that moment, Iraq had bombarded a school near my aunt's neighborhood. We were terrified. We couldn't do anything but listen to the radio repeating over and over: "Avoid that area. Avoid that area." We had no news from my aunt, but we could see the smoke rising from that direction.

Eventually, though I don't remember how, since I don't think we had a phone at home at that time, my aunt somehow got a message to us. She said the entire lunch she had prepared was covered in broken glass from the explosion. They told us they were going to come to our home instead because they were so scared. They came over, and my father was shaken, terrified.

That day, my father told all of us, including my aunt's family, that we should stay in a village until things became more stable. We listened. The next day, we left for a small village. I don't remember exactly how long we stayed there, but it was at least two weeks. It was calm there. The alarms never went off, but we constantly listened to the radio to find out what was happening in the cities.

Those of us who were school-aged decided to attend school in the village because we didn't know how long we would be there. And that was where I experienced something funny, something that wasn't bullying, at least not in the Western sense, but very common in the culture I grew up in.

The village students and the city students had this amusing, competitive dynamic. The classroom windows had metal fences across them, and the village kids would drag their hands across the metal to make a loud screeching sound, almost exactly like the sound of jets coming to bomb. It would scare us "city kids" to death at first, and then they would laugh. But they weren't mean; they were friendly. We became friends. It was just their little prank, something they did all the time to tease us and make us jump.

After a few weeks, we went back home, and the situation became a little more stable. And if I remember correctly, a few months after that, Iran and Iraq finally reached a peace agreement, and the war ended. It was good, of course, it brought relief, but by then, the damage had already been done. The war had already destroyed my childhood, the childhood of people my age in both Iran and Iraq, and there was no way to go back and rebuild what we had lost. War takes away things you can never recreate.

Sometimes I think that even the soldiers themselves are innocent people. They are influenced by propaganda, pushed into fighting human beings just like themselves. Then what really separates humans from animals? It's why I sometimes believe the most dangerous animal in the world is the human being. Deep inside, most of us do not want to kill each other. We want to live in peace, discover each other's cultures, and become friends. But politicians, the people in power, play their games for money and control, and ordinary people become victims.

They always say they want a "better life for their citizens," but the entire world is made of citizens of this planet. There is no difference between a child born in Iran and a child born in America; we don't choose where we are born. Yet the people in power choose whether we live in peace or grow up in fear.

And for me, that meant I never truly had a childhood.

My memories took me back to my teenage years. We were very close to my youngest uncle's family. They had only one daughter, and my younger sister and I would spend many days at their home. We slept over often, and some weeks we spent more days at my uncle's home than our own. My uncle was a truck driver, so he wasn't home most of the time. It was usually just me, my sister, my cousin, and my uncle's wife. She was sweet, incredibly kind, and she was a great cook as well. We were so close.

Then one day, my uncle's wife was in the hospital. The doctors said there was no hope. I was around twelve years old, in middle school, and I couldn't understand it. Why did this have to happen? My childhood had already been destroyed, and now, in my teenage years, someone I loved and adored so deeply was dying. I couldn't accept it. It was unbearably hard. But what could we do? Soon, she was gone.

Right after she passed away, I got sick again, this time with epilepsy. I had to go from one doctor to another. My father did everything he could. He took me to Tehran to see the best doctors. He took me to religious healers, holy Islamic sites, and prayer gatherings. At that time, I didn't really believe in any of it. I was going back and forth between being religious and not religious, but I did it because of my father, because he believed. We tried everything.

The epilepsy continued until my last year of high school. Because of it, I had to repeat the second year of middle school and the first year of high school.

In my high school years, after I fell in love with reading, I knew I wanted to be a writer or a journalist. That became my dream. So when the time came to choose a major, in Iran, high school students must choose a track; I chose Humanities. That was the field for future writers, journalists, and people interested in society. The other tracks were mathematics, technical trades that could lead to engineering, or medical sciences, but I knew what I wanted, so I chose Humanities.

I enrolled in a school called Amir Kabir, one of the better high schools in Zanjan at that time. I studied hard, but something happened that changed everything. Our school year wasn't divided into two semesters like in many places; we had three terms, and the exams in the third term were the most important ones. That was when my epilepsy was at its worst. Because of that, I couldn't attend several exams. I even remember in the middle of an exam, I had a seizure and had to be taken to the hospital. Because of all of this, I failed five or six classes that term.

Then something happened that made me angry, really angry. They invited my mother and me to the principal's office. Instead of telling me that I had failed several classes, they gave me gifts. They said I was one of the top students in my class.

But I knew the truth. I knew the gifts were not because of my success. They were because of my epilepsy, because they felt sorry for me. It wasn't recognition; it was compassion. I didn't want compassion. I don't like lies, and I especially didn't like being treated differently because of my sickness. Even back then, I wanted independence. I wanted people to see me for who I was, not for my illness. At that moment, although kind in its intention, it felt dishonest, and it stayed with me for a long time.

I didn't want to stay in that high school for one more day. I told my parents that I was going to study Metallurgy at a technical high school called Shaheed Motahari. So, I went and enrolled in that school. I started a new life and a new school year, and once again, I had to repeat the first year of high school. I wasn't happy about it, because it wasn't my passion. It wasn't what I wanted to do with my life. But at the same time, I couldn't handle that dishonesty, that compassion, that feeling of people being sorry for me. Because of that, I chose to start at this new school instead.

I was experiencing everything that comes with being a teenager, falling in love, getting my heart broken, and repeating the whole cycle again. I was also trying to build my mind and shape my personality. One day, I was very religious; the next day, I hated religion. Everything was confusing, and everything was happening all at once.

There isn't much to say about those four years because, truthfully, I hated them. I hated the field, but I still wanted to graduate and get my high school diploma. I told myself it was better than staying somewhere where people felt sorry for me, instead of encouraging me or giving me a real chance to retake the exams. So, I stayed, finished high school, and soon it was time to take the university entrance exam. In Iran, you must pass that exam to be accepted into a university, and it was incredibly difficult, extremely difficult. There were two parts to the exam. I passed the first one, and when I was preparing for the second one, another major change happened in my life.

I was preparing for the second university exam when one of my uncles passed away. Around the same time, my youngest uncle, the one I was extremely close to, had become deeply passionate about mountain climbing. He had already climbed Mount Damavand, and during that period, he also fell in love with reading history books. Because he had climbed Damavand, I bought him a book about the history of Iran as a gift. He was so happy. He told me, "When I come back from climbing Mount Alamkouh, I'll start reading this book. I'm going to enjoy it so much."

Mountain climbing had changed his life in a very positive way.

So, he left to climb Mount Alamkouh, and meanwhile, the date of my second university exam was getting closer and closer. Then one day we received news, vague news, that something had happened to my uncle, but no one would tell us what it was.

I went to my brother-in-law's shop, the only place nearby with a landline, and I tried calling the mountain climbers' camp. It wasn't a hotel or anything like that; it was just a simple building with shared rooms and a small commercial kitchen, a place where climbers stayed for a night before starting their ascent. I kept calling and calling. The phone rang and rang, but no one answered. Finally, when someone picked up, they said they didn't know anything.

I went back home, and the first person I saw was my aunt, among my uncles. She was crying so hard, uncontrollably. I asked her what happened, and she hugged me tightly and said, "Your uncle... my brother... is gone."

We all broke down. We all loved him so much, and losing him hit our entire family like an earthquake.

After that, I completely stopped preparing for the second exam. On the day of the exam, at noon, the mountain climbers were going to leave Zanjan to climb Mount Alamkouh in memory of my uncle, and I desperately wanted to join them. So, during the exam, I didn't really pay attention. It was multiple choice, so I just marked whatever answers seemed right so I could leave quickly and join the climbers.

Naturally, I failed that exam.

Since I couldn't pass the exam, by law I had to go to the military and serve for two years. Even if you go to university, you still have to serve, but you can go after graduation, and you serve as an officer. With only a high school diploma, you go as a sergeant. So, I went to the military.

I really don't like talking about that time because, to me, it was a complete waste. I didn't gain anything meaningful from it, other than a few friendships. People in Iran always say that military service "shapes a man's life" because it's difficult. I'm not saying it wasn't difficult, but honestly, I had far tougher days mountain climbing than I ever had in the military.

I truly hated it. It wasn't meaningful, there was nothing valuable to learn, and I never felt it added anything to my life. Yes, I made a few memories, and I did make some friends. We visited each other's cities, and they visited mine, but even with that, it still wasn't a bright or even good period of my life. I just never liked the military, and because of that, I don't really wish to talk about that time at all.

After the military, I found a job in the biggest factory in my city, Zanjan. The factory was called Iran Transfo. They made transfer motors, and I got hired as a welder. Right after finishing my service, I started working there. It felt good to have a job, and of course, it wasn't my first work experience. I have been working since I was nine years old.

After school, I would go straight to my father's small shop. He sold hardware tools, a tiny shop, nothing like the big hardware stores you see in the Western world. My father would bring lunch for me, give me an hour to eat and finish my homework, and then I had to help him in the shop until evening. We closed the shop together and walked home. And on some Fridays, our only weekend in Iran, about once every few months, he would take me with him to do a deep cleaning of the shop. That was my childhood: school, work, home.

So working wasn't new to me. But starting a full-time job as a welder was different. I hated that job so much because it wasn't my passion. My childhood dream was still with me: I wanted to be a journalist, a teacher, or a writer. Welding didn't make me happy. The only good part was the pay; it was decent, and I could have a comfortable life with that income.

I remember my very first paycheck. I did two things: first, I went to the pastry shop and bought two kilograms of pastries for my family. Second, I bought a washing machine for my mom. Being able to do that made me so happy.

I stayed in that job for five years, until the day everything changed.

I was walking on the main street in Zanjan, the one called Chaharrah to Saadi Vasat, when I saw an advertisement: the first daily newspaper of Zanjan was hiring. It immediately caught my eye, and I said to myself, this is it.

I applied, even though I had almost no real experience, just a little work I had recently started for a weekly newspaper in Zanjan. I used to write articles about sports there, mostly because I had become a mountain climber, so I handled the sports pages for that weekly paper. It wasn't professional at all; I never had any training. I would just write articles, gather some news, and put everything together.

But this new opportunity felt different. It felt serious, professional, exactly what I wanted. So, I applied, went to the interview, and got accepted. They told us we would have six months of unpaid training.

Somehow, I managed to continue working at Iran Transfo while attending the newspaper training sessions. But the day came when I couldn't manage to work at both places anymore. I had to make a decision.

On one hand, I knew I was about to leave a well-paid job with stability. On the other hand, I knew I was finally getting closer to my dream.

I decided to follow my dream.

I quit my job at Iran Transfo, and I remember almost everyone, except my classmates at the newspaper training, calling me stupid. Iran Transfo was well-known for good pay and great benefits, and they couldn't understand why I would leave all of that for six months of unpaid work. They'd say, "You're crazy. Journalists in Iran barely get paid anything."

But I didn't listen to anyone. I wanted to follow my passion and my dream. So, I did.

Two things during this time changed my life forever. The first was the very first article I wrote. It was an interview with the first local principal of a high school in Zanjan who was now living in Tehran. I traveled to Tehran to interview him for the newspaper, and when I returned, I wrote the introduction, the opening entry, for the piece. The Q&A part was fine, but the intro needed to be written separately.

When I handed it to one of my editors, he tore it up and said it was garbage. I was furious. I asked him why he tore it apart instead of giving me the chance to revise it, and he just said, "No. It was garbage. Write something completely different."

This continued, four or five times, if I remember correctly. Each time, he tore it up again. Finally, he said, "I need a drink," and I said okay. After we had a drink, I sat down and rewrote the introduction. This time, he loved it. He joked, "From now on, whenever you want to write, you should drink." Of course, it was a joke; I never did that again, but the important part is this: he made me a better journalist. He made me a better writer. His harshness came from wanting a good result, and I have never forgotten what he did for me.

The second thing that changed my life happened one day when I said aloud that I really wanted to go to Tehran and work for the big newspapers. One of my editors looked at me and said, "There is no 'someday.' You're going tomorrow night."

It was a Thursday. I laughed and said, "No, I can't go. I need to prepare. I need to find a place to live, find a job, figure things out."

He said, "No. You already decided. You're going."

Then he called a mutual friend right in front of me and said, "Hamid is coming to Tehran. Can you find him a job?"

That friend replied, "Actually, there's already a job waiting for him at a news agency."

And that was it.

Friday night, at midnight, I got on a bus at 4 a.m., and I arrived in Tehran. I went straight to the office of the news agency. As soon as I arrived, they handed me a few reports to work on. At the same time, I began looking for a place to stay, so I called my mountain-climbing coach. I knew his brother lived in Tehran and might be able to help.

My coach called his brother, and within a short time, the brother called me. He said he had just finished building an apartment complex, and one of the units was empty. "There's nothing in it," he said. "No furniture. Nothing except a kettle and a propane gas stove."

I told him, "That's okay. I'll stay there."

In the evening, after work, I took a bus to the place my mountain-climbing coach's brother had offered me. When I arrived, I found a piece of cardboard and used it as a mattress. I didn't have anything else, just a small bag with a few pieces of clothing. I went out, bought some bread and cheese for dinner, and that was it for my first night.

The next morning, because there was no water heater or anything in the apartment, I boiled water in the kettle and used it to take a shower. My folded clothes became my pillow. I didn't have a blanket, a bed, or even a proper chair. That was my entire life in that empty apartment.

I stayed there for about a week, working during the day and returning to that bare room at night. When the weekend came, I went back to Zanjan to gather a pillow, a blanket, and a few basic things to make life a little easier.

I stayed in that place for two more weeks, until the same person told me that he had just bought an old building he planned to demolish in a few months. He said it had a kitchen, a water heater, and a shower, basic things I didn't have, and told me I could live there if I wanted. The only condition was that the Afghan workers who worked for him were living on one floor, and I could take the second floor. I didn't care about any of that. I was just grateful.

I thanked him, moved into the old building, and then traveled back to Zanjan again to bring the rest of my belongings, my bed, and whatever else I had. My nephew helped me load everything into his truck and drive it to Tehran. And that's how I started my new life in that old building.

The building had two floors of the same size. On the first floor, there were about thirteen Afghan workers living together in that small space. I insisted that some of them move upstairs and share the second floor with me. We all worked during the day and only needed a place to sleep at night, and it didn't seem fair that they were all crowded into one room while I stayed alone upstairs.

But they were so respectful, mindful, polite, and genuinely amazing people. They kept saying, "No, no, we won't bother you. We get up very early in the morning, and we don't want to disturb you." No matter how much I encouraged them, they refused out of respect, so they continued living downstairs, and I continued living alone on the second floor.

I remember when my dad and mom came to Tehran because I needed to take my father to a doctor's appointment. Whenever the Afghans heard my parents walking downstairs toward the bathroom, they wouldn't come out at all. They didn't want to make my parents uncomfortable in any way. I was so impressed by how respectful they were. Because of that, we became very good friends.

I always wish I could find them again, especially the one who was the leader of the group. His name was Reza. I truly hope one day I can reconnect with him. He was one of the sweetest, kindest people I have ever met in my entire life.

My dream had finally come true. At the same time I was going to college for journalism, I was writing articles for major newspapers, the kind I had always admired. But it was frustrating and exhausting. Day after day, the government would shut down one newspaper, and we would have to move to another. Then a week later, that paper would get shut down too, and we would have to move again. It was chaos. It was discouraging. But we still had hope. We hoped things would eventually change, so we kept fighting by writing.

I never wrote political articles. I focused only on social issues. But the Iranian government, in its paranoia, was extremely sensitive even about social topics. They were even sensitive about sports articles. It was ridiculous. Because of this, I kept losing job after job, not just me, but all my colleagues. And the pay was terrible. If my mother didn't send food from Zanjan, I would often have nothing to eat. All I could afford was my rent, nothing more.

Still, I continued. I kept writing until the first major union after the Islamic Revolution began forming in Iran, the Public Transportation Bus Drivers Union. The government became incredibly sensitive about that union, and I was the journalist covering their news. One day, authorities ordered the newspaper I worked for to fire me, or they would shut the entire paper down.

My editor told me everything. I didn't want the newspaper to suffer because of me, so I left voluntarily. But it seemed the government didn't stop there. They warned other newspapers not to publish any article with my name either.

I had no choice but to leave Tehran. After two years of trying to build a life there, I returned to Zanjan to live with my parents again.

I knew only one place I could return to and possibly work again: the first newspaper that had hired me, the daily paper in Zanjan. I went there, and the owner asked to speak with me. He told me he was willing to keep me and even pay me, but only under one condition: I could gather online news and send it to the editors, but I could no longer write. He said the Iranian regime had informed him that I was banned from writing, even under a different name.

He wanted to help me, and this was the only way he could do it. I accepted, but my income was barely enough to survive until the middle of the month. After that, I had nothing, even though I was living with my parents again in my small room in the basement. Still, that was the only way I could stay at that newspaper.

When Staying Was No Longer Living

All of this eventually pushed me to think more seriously about leaving, about moving on, leaving my country, my home, and the thirty-one years of memories I had built in Iran.

This last stretch of time in Niğde was spent entirely in my memories. It was like replaying my entire life on a loop: childhood in Zanjan, teenage years, my early adulthood, journalism, the mountains, my family, my friends, Iran, Turkey, everything.

It continued like that until the day finally came, the day I had to leave Niğde and travel to Istanbul for my final days in Turkey.

I wanted to go to Istanbul a week earlier and spend a few days there with two of my best friends, Majid and Hossein, who were coming from Iran to see me before I left Turkey for the U.S. My family was overjoyed that, finally, all the waiting was over and I was heading to my final destination. I could hardly believe it, coming from the south side of Zanjan, an area mostly for poor people, in a small city, I was about to live in one of the largest countries in the world, a place many people dream of living in.

I went to the police station to request permission to leave a week early. They told me that they could only give me permission 48 hours before my flight. I pleaded, explaining my wish to go early, and they eventually agreed. At that time, Turkish law required refugees leaving the country to pay a fee for the time they had spent in Turkey. I don't remember the exact term they used, but it was essentially a "residency fee."

I remembered that during Nowruz, the Iranian New Year celebrated in Iran, Azerbaijan, and parts of Turkey, the Turkish Prime Minister had said something in his speech about the unity of nations: "We are one nation under seven different governments." When the officers at the police station mentioned the fee, I jokingly said, "Do you know Abdullah Gül? He said in Nowruz that we are one nation under seven governments. Do you really want money from your own nation?" They laughed so hard that one of them fell to the ground, and their boss came in to see what was happening.

After hearing the story, she smiled and said, "You must be Hamid, right?" I confirmed, and she said, "Yes, you're really a journalist. You know how to use words in the right place." We all laughed, and finally, the officers agreed that I only needed to cover a small part of the fee, just enough to buy some ink for their printers. I happily bought it for them and returned it. By the time I came back, they had stamped my documents permitting me to leave Niğde.

I bought my last bus ticket from Niğde to Istanbul. At the bus station, people I had helped, whether with translation or finding a place to rent, were there to see me off. They brought gifts, and the moment was both sweet and bittersweet. I felt joy that I was finally leaving for my final destination, but I also felt sadness for those still waiting, the ones without interview dates, and Majid, whose case had been denied and was waiting for an appeal.

After saying my goodbyes, I took the bus to Istanbul, where Majid and Hossein were waiting for me. We spent my last days in Turkey together, visiting different places in Istanbul, enjoying food and drinks, exploring islands, and sharing unforgettable moments. They even bought me some thoughtful gifts.

With Hossein and Majid, Istanbul was pure joy. Every day was laughter, reliving old memories from Iran, whether in the mountains, in forests, or out in nature; from the time Majid and I were both in Tehran; from Hossein's visits to Zanjan; or when I traveled to Hamadan to be with him and his family. Every single day was light, laughter, and an ease that felt rare and precious.

One night, we were walking along Istiklal Caddesi (Istiklal Street), crowded and alive, slick with rain. I had done a bit of shopping, and suddenly the January rain came down hard, cold, and relentless. I didn't want shelter. I wanted the rain. I wanted to be soaked, to feel it all. I remember Hossein laughing and taking photos of me as I walked like a mad person through the storm, drenched and laughing uncontrollably. In that moment, wet and freezing and alive, I felt something simple and powerful: joy without fear, laughter without permission, and a freedom I didn't yet know how much I would need to remember.

Toward the Land of Dreams

Finally, the day arrived: January 14, 2010. As dawn broke, my plane rose into the sky, carrying my hopes, my fears, and my future toward the land of dreams.

About the Author

Hamid Ran was born in 1976 in Zanjan, Iran. He spent most of his life there before becoming a journalist and moving to Tehran to pursue his career with major newspapers and news agencies.

Because of his journalistic work, he was forced to leave Iran after coming under pressure from the Ministry of Intelligence. In 2008, he left the country for Turkey and applied for refugee status through the United Nations. In 2010, after his refugee case was fully approved by both the United Nations and the United States, he resettled in the U.S.

He first lived in Maryland and Virginia before working as a reporter in Washington, D.C. for an Iranian television network. After the network shut down, and without sufficient English skills at the time to continue in journalism, he relocated to Dallas, Texas. There, he attended college English as a Second Language and general studies courses while working to support himself.

In 2016, he moved to Colorado and transitioned into the human services field, bringing with him his own experience as a refugee. He worked at a refugee resettlement agency, first as a caseworker and later as a caseworker supervisor, helping other refugees navigate the unknowns of resettlement and rebuild their lives. He now lives in Colorado, continues his work in human services, and pursues his creative work as a writer and photographer.

An Explanation That I Owe

If your name is not in this book, it does not mean that I did not care about you or that I forgot you. The only reason I did not name friends who are still in Iran was to avoid any possible harm to them. For this, I owe you an apology. You were truly among those who touched my life, and you are one of the reasons I am here today, living a life outside of Iran. My heart and my thoughts are with you. I think of you often, and I hope that one day we will see each other again, to talk, laugh, and cry, just as we did in Iran. I am waiting for that day.